Church Growth That Counts

Church Growth That Counts

Ralph H. Elliott

Judson Press ® Valley Forge

CHURCH GROWTH THAT COUNTS

Copyright © 1982
Judson Press, Valley Forge, PA 19481

Library of Congress Cataloging in Publication Data

Elliott, Ralph H.
  Church growth that counts.

  Includes bibliographical references.
  1. Church growth.   I. Title.
BV652.25.E44   254'.5   81-13670
ISBN 0-8170-0943-4   AACR2

Dedicated to
EARL A. ELLIOTT
—who, as my father,
is truly a "quiet"
man in the
biblical sense—

And to
NORTH SHORE BAPTIST CHURCH,
Chicago, Illinois
—a community of
faith with unity
in diversity—

Acknowledgments

I am grateful to my staff colleagues at North Shore Baptist Church for their understanding in caring for some of my duties while I wrote this book. Mrs. Mildred O. Chapman, my secretary, was especially helpful in typing the manuscript. It was the director of North Shore's Counseling Program, Dr. H. Rhea Gray, who first acquainted me with the six functional areas of ministry that appear under "The Shape of the Local Parish." Appreciation is expressed to Ms. Phyllis A. Frantz, manuscript editor at Judson Press, for being helpful in so many ways.

Contents

Introduction:
A Setting and a Hope

I serve a church whose building has been located in the Uptown-Edge-water section of the city of Chicago for seventy-five years. Draw a picture of the church in the city, almost anywhere in the United States, and you will draw the cultural and sociological pattern of our environment, except that ours is probably more intense.

In the early days of the church the community was one of single-family units of the middle-class and upper-middle-class variety. During the days of World War II, war needs brought to the city a large number of Appalachian whites. Many of them settled in our area in the hotels and homes that were divided and subdivided again to create multiple housing units. That phase passed, and the next wave was a multi-Asian and Hispanic constituency. Once again the church sought to adjust to a changing community and a changing constituency. The large Anglo (Caucasian) congregation, partly from paternalism and partly from a genuine sense of mission, sought to minister to the new residents. An intentional effort was made to reach the new residents. There was some degree of success, and as early as the 1950s, Chinese, Japanese, and Hispanic worship opportunities were provided. Today we are a church of multiple congregations—Anglo, Chinese, Filipino, Hispanic, and Japanese. These are not "churches" using "our" building. All of the people are members of North Shore Baptist Church. Many of the activities and ministries of the church are participated in with pluralistic support. Except on occasions of great celebration, the worship life remains separate, in various parts of the building at various times, and is for the most part conducted by appropriate language ministers. There is much excitement as we celebrate our larger family composed of so many diverse elements. We often sound the note that "God has made of one blood all peoples to dwell upon the face of the earth" (see Acts 17:26). Long-range planning has created a coordinating council whose task is calendar building and building use assignment. Each group within the church is represented on the council on an equal basis.

The church represents, in microcosm, the community in which it is situated. The nearby high school is probably the most racially mixed of any school in the city of Chicago—maybe of any in the country. Some fifty-plus national groups are represented in its student body. Believing that a church should serve the people in its geographical community, the congregants have worked long and hard to build an inclusive community. On a practical matter of strategy, it is not possible for the church to be a white church or black or Chinese or Filipino or Hispanic or Japanese or whatever because none of these constitutes the major part of the community. All live together, side by side, street after street.

Things seemed to go well in earlier years when the Anglos were of sufficient numerical strength to carry the major financial weight of the larger program. In more recent years as the Anglo group has become smaller, it has become very obvious that we need better thought-out patterns of growth and outreach. We are faced with all of the problems and opportunities that urbanologists and sociologists have been writing about for years. The denomination of which we are a part still leans upon us as one of the strongest contributors to its national budget. Yet in spite of growth in inclusiveness and an exciting pluralistic family, we have been in a state of serious numerical decline since the mid-1950s.

Then out of nowhere came what appeared to be the promised salvation, the church growth movement. I eagerly began reading its literature in a quest for insights, methods, and programs. The reports of its numerical success were exciting.

"Church growth" is a technical phrase for a philosophy and a methodology that have their source and setting in the School of World Mission and Institute of Church Growth at Fuller Theological Seminary in California. The work attempts "to apply the scientific principles of church growth as developed by Donald McGavran specifically to the American scene."[1] It was introduced to the United States in 1972 by McGavran and is based on the fruit of his work as a third-generation missionary to India, where he served for thirty years. He created the Institute of Church Growth, first at Northwest Christian College in Eugene, Oregon, and later in larger form at Fuller Theological Seminary. McGavran's book *Understanding Church Growth*[2] is considered the Magna Carta of the church growth movement. Presently the primary spokesmen for the movement are two of McGavran's protégés, Win C. Arn and C. Peter Wagner. One of its popularizers is Robert Schuller of Garden Grove Community Church in California (the "crystal cathedral"), whose book *Your Church Has Real Possibilities*[3] is portrayed as one "of the finest case studies of growing churches in America."[4]

A whole cadre of church growth professionals has grown up, and they are flooding the country with institutes and seminars. The success illustrations are such churches as Coral Ridge Presbyterian, Florida; Redwood Chapel in Castro Valley, California; First Nazarene in Denver; First Baptist of Hammond, Indiana; Thomas Road Baptist Church in Lynchburg, Virginia (Jerry Falwell of Moral Majority fame); and First Baptist in Dallas. The so-called "electronic church" is an extension of church growth techniques, the marketing techniques of capitalism's success patterns. This formalized philosophy is now filtering into every denomination in America. Desperately declining main-line groups like United Presbyterians, Episcopalians, Methodists, and American Baptists are giving listening ears, and various seminaries appear to view the movement as the answer to everything.

I turned to the movement for possible help and vociferously devoured its many books and publications. My attitude has moved from hope, to fascination, to alarm, to disgust, to fairness, to seeing the possibility of some eclectic borrowing of some aspects if they are carefully moderated and controlled by biblical and theological maturity. The theological persuasion of the heart of the movement is so different from my own (it ranges from conservative to fundamentalist) that I increasingly studied its literature with a chip on my shoulder. I have had to look at this movement primarily from the vantage point of my own individual roots and experiences and especially from the setting where I presently serve as a pastor, seeking some answers. My experiential journey has led from the isolationism of Southern Baptist life where I was disenfranchised as a seminary professor in 1962[5] to the ecumenical growth of the post-Vatican II period when my perception of the Christian family was considerably changed through teaching assignments in a Roman Catholic college and seminary, to my involvement with the pluralistic life of three urban settings—Albany and metropolitan New York and Chicago.

The kind of church of which I am presently a part leads me to view with alarm the basic thesis of the church growth movement. That thesis is that churches must be built with homogeneous people only. A higher rate of conversion growth can be predicted for the homogeneous church. Therefore, it is important that a church be composed of basically one kind of people where folk "feel at home" and know they are among "our kind of people." Over and over the literature stresses that "men like to become Christians without crossing racial, linguistic, or class barriers."[6] This view contrasts with the very understanding of the church as being inclusive of all people, as they are represented in the community of which I am a part. At the same time, case study records make it clear that the church growth philosophy and methodology obviously succeed in building a "religious institution." Its greatest danger may be that it obviously succeeds.

At the same time I am intrigued by the constant suggestion that growth is a matter of attitude.[7] This intrigue is matched by my discontent with the "rationale for smallness" so frequently encountered within main-line denominations. Most of us in main-line and liberal churches have used a "remnant" theology for so long as a justification for our failure to grow that we have lost the motivation to be Christ's evangels. In our defensive posturing we have been guilty of some faulty logic. I agree, for instance, with the major thrust of Robert K. Hudnut's little book *Church Growth Is Not the Point,* but I certainly do not, as he does, see it as a good sign that people are leaving the churches. Nor would I, as does he, rationalize that "loss of growth in statistics has often meant increase in growth in the Gospel."[8] I cannot even be sure that what we have left is the faithful remnant.

The need of the institution that I serve and my personal need and ambivalence have thus led me through several phases of work, which I propose to share.

It was impossible for me to evaluate what I was finding in church growth without developing "A Theology of Church and Mission." This is an attempt to demonstrate that "church" as the people of God is a phenomenon with roots in the Old Testament and continuity through the New Testament pattern. I will try to point out the diversity within the people of God, even from the earliest days of the confederated or associated tribal settings. The struggles of the Jewish-Gentile Christian world further developed diversity as being the ideal—an accepting community inclusive of all.

"An Analysis of Church Growth in Light of a Theological Understanding of the Church" is the next step. Here I will focus upon the primary tenets of the movement as presented through the church growth materials. The purpose of this section is to outline the major emphases and tentatively to relate them to the contextual atmosphere of the previous section. My task in "An Evaluation of the Church Growth Movement" is to build further and demonstrate the strengths and weaknesses of the basic tenets with a keen eye cast upon their shortcomings. I intend to indicate that although there are many insights that we need to borrow from church growth, the movement is very inadequate, especially as related to liberation concerns and the needs of dispossessed peoples. Both of the above parts, the analyses and the evaluation of church growth, are closely related.

I have both learned and experienced something in my study of church growth, however. Tentative and timid beginnings are projected in "A Positive Ministry for Growth." Brief gleanings from Dietrich Bonhoeffer will furnish both positive and negative guidelines to keep us on the right track. "The Shape of the Local Parish" is directly related. Here I will try to look at some structures of church which come from a biblical under-standing and attempt to indicate their relevance for "being the church" where we are just now, with particular concern for the urban church. The assumption is that what urban churches face is but a microcosm of what all churches will face as the suburban rings continue to age and develop many of the same problems/opportunities.

1

A Theology of Church and Mission

W hat is the biblical basis of church? From the first to the last the Bible is concerned with God's purpose in creating a people for himself, or as Peter summarized what he had borrowed from the Book of Exodus, 19:5-6: "You are a chosen group, a royal priesthood, a holy nation, God's own people, that you may declare the wonderful deeds of him who called you out of darkness into his marvelous light" (1 Peter 2:9). Three specific verses in this Petrine epistle (1 Peter 2:8-10) describe the church (the body of believers) in terms of Israel as the holy people of God. The church is the church when she recognizes that she is the people of God.

The church, with her roots deep in the Old Testament, has been called into being by two acts of God—the salvation event of Exodus in the Old Testament and the redemption event of Christ in the New Testament.

That there is continuity of thought and development in the Old and New Testaments is readily recognized. Stephen unflinchingly referred to the church *(ecclesia)* as belonging to the wilderness period and spoke of Moses in relationship to that church (Acts 7:38). This assumed continuity may partially account for the lack of explicit reference to the church in the teachings of Jesus. If Jesus used the term "church" at all, it is recorded on only two occasions and both in the ecclesiastical Gospel of Matthew. To suggest that the omission of church references by the Gospel writers is due to the church being only a post-resurrection creation is to deny both continuity and the people of God concept.

Whatever the time frame of the church, she is always a special creation of people for God, elected to special ministry for God in behalf of *all* humanity and addressing herself to *all* humanity. Even as God did not call Abraham just to be Abraham or Jacob just to be Jacob or the twelve disciples just to be twelve disciples but to become the people of God, so God did not call the people of God to privilege but to privileged responsibility.

It is most important to recognize that this creation of a people of God had the world and all its peoples as a backdrop. The peoples to be addressed in the formation of a covenant people are all the peoples of the world in their heterogeneous variety. The first eleven chapters of Genesis are a portrayal of all of humankind (summarized in "the international table" of Genesis 10). It was to them, not just to the people of "our kind," that Israel was to address its message as a covenant people. The first Hebrew people were called to live and work in a strange and alien culture. Abraham had to leave, not bless, his home culture. Israel's failure to be inclusive in terms of its challenge was a prelude to disaster. Aliens and strangers were to be given a secure place. Those who were not "our kind" were invited to have a place in the ministry itself. "Come with us, and we will do you good" (Numbers 10:29) was the open call to those who were not "our kind." In that better day of the kingdom when Zion recaptures her glory, people of all kinds will flow there together in the worship of God. Gentiles and Jews and animals of varying kinds will associate together in harmony and peace (Isaiah 9:1-2; 11:6-9).

Conditions Necessitating the Event

The nature of the church is rooted in the theology of Genesis. The church was the ultimate form that evolved from the covenant response to the need stated in the theological introduction, Genesis 1–10.

Rooted in the sovereignty of God and in the intended fellowship between God and people, humankind's particular responsibility was to "image" or represent God throughout the created order (Genesis 1–2). *Elohim* (God) and the basic word for deity in chapter 1 suggests sovereignty and authority, the essence of the root meaning of the word. Human creation is thus dependent upon a sovereign God. *Yahweh* (LORD), the basic word for deity in Genesis 2:4*b,* suggests an intimate and personal relationship since the word occurs time and again in a fellowship setting. Human responsibility is to enter into relationship with and to represent (*image*—Genesis 1:27) the transcendent yet imminent God, who is both far away and very near.

Unfortunately, the experience of humankind is that we ever and again seek to be the masters of our own fate, the captains of our souls, fall into the temptation to usurp the place of God, represent ourselves alone, and clamor for a place under the sun (see Genesis 1–11). Such is the experience of Everyman and Everywoman. When this happens within the human spirit, when self-centeredness takes over, we find ourselves shut out of the paradisical relationship which God intended and denied the very life that we sought ("shut out of the garden" parabolically). Inevitably, having violated our relationship with God and in a position of disharmony with God, we then fall into disharmony with our brothers and sisters. To murder our relationship with God results in murdering our relationship with our brother, as depicted in the Cain and Abel narrative (Genesis 4). The vertical and horizontal relationships (if we may use spatial terms) always go together. The fragmentation of community (Genesis 11) goes hand in hand with the fragmentation of the God relationship.

It is important to note that Genesis 10 portrays the nations as existing together in harmony. Genesis 11 is a picture of separated nations, and such fragmentation is a violation of the God-desired "given." It is not until the day of Pentecost experience in Acts 2 that we have a biblical picture of the reversal of the Tower of Babel experience. Pentecost and not Babel is the biblical norm. Therefore, it appears strange to me that the church growth people should argue so stringently for separation! One will readily agree that it may initially be easier to work with homogeneous peoples rather than heterogeneous ones, but that hardly appears to be a mandate, and it certainly is counter to the biblical ideal.

It is the sinful condition of humankind that separates us. Our need is for reconciliation. God intended that we should be one people with a vibrant, beautiful life, an available life as is represented by the tree placed in the midst of the garden. Other nonbiblical creation accounts picture the tree of life outside the garden, reserved for the gods but unavailable to the lowly human. Meaningful life, however, must come through God-given experiences. It is not self-produced, something that we can reach out and get apart from the divine-human relationship. Although the church growth people do not intend to have a disunity between divine spirit and human methodology, the constant emphasis that a church will succeed if it uses the right methodology is perilously near to the Genesis sin.

Recognizing these early chapters in Genesis as giving a theological preface in story form, we know that the universal experience is to miss the intentionality of God. What follows is a portrayal of God's answer to human need. The initiation of covenant rescue (bringing people back to God and back to one another) through the election-call of a people (Genesis 11:31–50:26) is the sowing of the seed that grows toward completion in the remainder of the biblical story, both in the Old and New Testaments. Not willing to cast creation aside nor to leave it in disunion, God chooses a segment of humankind to speak to all of humankind in God's behalf (Genesis 12:2-3). This elected people (church) is never called primarily for itself but to speak in behalf of another for the sake of others. The maintenance of the privileged relationship is dependent upon a willingness to lean on God (Genesis 15:6) and even to sacrifice to that end one's Isaac, whatever that Isaac might be (Genesis 22). The continuity and perseverance of God's plan for the "church" is conveyed through the vehicle of the patriarchal narratives. However, this initiation of a churchly people awaits formalization as a covenant people as a result of the great Exodus event. The call to be a missionary people is authenticated by that event.

Claims That the Event Makes

The key for any characterization of church or people of God is the section known as the "Book of the Covenant," Exodus 19–24; this material provided a primary setting for the New Testament understanding of the church in 1 Peter 2:8-10.

Although there have been elaborations and modifications, George Mendenhall's *Law and Covenant in Israel and the Ancient Near East*[1] continues to be basic for understanding covenant development. For the sake of brevity, we will use the trilogy of prelude (Exodus 19), stipulations (Exodus 20–23), and ratification (Exodus 24) as the summary poles. Anyone familiar with Mendenhall's work recognizes that these three "poles" have been pulled from an elaborate Hittite covenant-making background and that this background greatly influenced the *forms* in which the peculiar *theology* is presented.

Prelude

The biblical covenant is not a contract or bargain between equals (a parity covenant). It is a will in which a sovereign will maker, from his own grace and goodness, wills to give a particular inheritance or assignment to a people. Certain claims are connected with the will, claims based upon certain actions of the will maker, i.e., actions authenticating the will. This latter is known as a "suzerainty" covenant.

In this instance, God is the will maker who makes certain claims upon Israel, the recipient of the will. God's delivering action in the Exodus event (Exodus 19:4) is the basis of God's right to make such a claim. The claim is that these people shall recognize a particular relationship (19:5) and serve in a particular role (19:6).

The elect are a "peculiar" people, or treasure, in the midst of all peoples. All are God's people, but these are chosen for a unique and particular use or function, just as a farmer who owns a huge farm may select a portion of his acreage for a particular use. This particular people of God are to live in the midst of all people of God as a living demonstration of wholeness, serving as a "kingdom of priests and a holy nation" (19:6). The people of God are holy (i.e., distinct, different, set apart, unique) in order that they may serve as "priest," i.e., as bridgebuilder, go-between, intermediary, or negotiator. Their uniqueness lies in the fact that theirs is a faith relationship and a moral relationship rather than merely a racial or ethnic relationship. That the people are "other" than those about them makes it possible for Israel to serve as the people of God in order that she may aid in building a bridge between God and humankind and *vice versa*. This is the essence of the church's purpose at any stage in her history.

Stipulations

This privileged relationship is based upon the fulfillment of certain conditions or stipulations, as is usually true of a will or covenant. The principles within the stipulations (Exodus 20:1-17) give birth to certain applications of the principles within certain situations and circumstances (20:18–23:33). The principles of the relationship are always the same. The application of those principles to specific and changing situations must be worked out by the people in the relationship. Regardless of the circumstances, people who have entered into a peculiar relationship with God (19:8) will always keep that profession with consistency (20:7). To claim to be the people of God and to live as though they were not is the greatest profanity. This so-called "commandment" (20:7) is a summary of the intent of all of the ten principles and forbids profession without consistency.

The import of the above which has relevance for our concern with church growth is that the people of God build a kind of community that achieves characteristics that are impossible for those who have not accepted God as will maker.

Ratification

In a covenant (will) ceremony in Exodus 24:1-6, God as the will maker and the people as recipients are joined together in one blood, i.e., one life, intent, and purpose.

Although political purpose and style ultimately obscured this theological understanding in Israel, it was never forgotten. It is remembered (Jeremiah 31), if even by a minority, that God purposes for himself a covenant community whose members have a relationship to God and to one another in experiencing and interpreting divine principle. A people do not have a relationship with God and remain separated from one another.

Continuity of Event and Claim in the New Testament

The heart of the Transfiguration experience portrays Jesus as speaking of ". . . his [exodus], which he was to accomplish at Jerusalem" (Luke 9:31). In this setting with Moses and Elijah it is suggested that the partial deliverance of God's people wrought by God at the first Exodus is now to be completed in the new exodus of crucifixion and resurrection. Here the Exodus and Christ experiences are definitely connected.

The same connection is made in the Lord's Supper experience (Matthew 26:28; Mark 14:24; Luke 22:20; 1 Corinthians 11:25). In all of these sources the blood of the new covenant has obvious reference to the blood of the old covenant (Exodus 24:8) and presents the Jesus experience as a formal rite that establishes a new covenant relationship. Analogous to the Mosaic covenant, the Lord's Supper establishes a lasting relationship between the community and Christ. In passing, let it be noted that "life . . . is in the blood" (Leviticus 17:11). To be joined in the blood of Christ is to be joined into one life. The Lord's table is not a segregated table.

Even as Jesus ties the formal Exodus covenant to Moses, so Paul ties the initial covenant of Abraham to Christ (Galatians 3:16). Likewise, the book of Hebrews is wholly based on the covenant pattern of the Old Testament and presents that pattern and purpose as fully fulfilled in the new Christian community. It is hard to escape the conclusion that the Old Testament (covenant) and the New Testament (covenant) in Christ's blood are one, as are the people one. Each of the covenants created a people of God who were to be in community with him for the purpose of calling others into relationship.

Even the fivefold structure of Matthew's Gospel with its stereotyped formula (7:28; 11:1; 13:53; 19:1; 26:1) points to the new community as being in continuity with earlier Mosaic days. Jesus is the new Moses, leading a new exodus, creating a new Israel, and engaging in a new mission. What the Exodus event of the Old Testament was in authenticating the divine will in calling into being a people of God, so the Christ event of incarnation, crucifixion, and resurrection is to the New Testament in calling into being a people of God. It is quite clear that these new people are a new creation (2 Corinthians 5:17). We are neither Jew nor non-Jew, Greek nor non-Greek, but a new creation, a third humanity. Likewise, what the stipulations of the ten words (Exodus 20) are in providing the moral substance of the life of the people of God, so the content of the Sermon on the Mount (Matthew 5–7) is to the people of God in the New Testament. Radical transformation of the usual ways and patterns of culture is the expectation. Although more will be said about this in the later analysis of the church growth movement, let it be noticed here that Gentile proselytes were under the influence of and included in the Exodus community emphasis and Hebrew disciples were included in the Sermon on the Mount community emphasis, often as part of the same community.

The contribution of biblical history suggests that the church is always related to a specific people of God who have a peculiar vision that motivates them to ministry. In the people-of-God/church theme, there is continuity across the testaments of a people with a vision claiming an allegiance that is superior to any other relationships.

Necessity of New Motivation

At times the organizational form and group self-centeredness of the people of God can hide their mission, and the purpose of being a called people is denied. Vision is domesticated, and some alternative consciousness is needed to energize the organization. There comes a time when the covenantal tradition of Moses must be recaptured. Ever and again, as in the time of Solomon, it is assumed that the character of God is "domiciled" at the royal parish and people must "come and get it"; and sometimes it is assumed that only certain ones are eligible. And if a people do have the vision, is the sharing of that vision confined primarily or only to a narrow geographical or "parish" area? Is "community" in Christian life circumscribed by geography, or is it based more on commonality of experience? There have always been those Christian groups who have found the visible expression of the church in the world as more experiential than geographical. From earliest days people from great distances came together to form the church in a local congregational expression—a "company of faithful people . . . who consent to walk together." Freedom to associate where they would was an outgrowth of the concept of freedom from political entities creating "parish" or "church."

Does this discipleship in terms of Christian community have any implication for us now? Usually in church planning, we begin by drawing concentric rings as though the "church" is to be composed of those in an immediate geographical area. Does this suggest that we are unduly influenced by the "parish" concept, and is it consistent with our history and understanding? There seems to be an assumption that the urban church is doomed to decay and demise as people move further from center city. Even denominational position papers are based on this premise. Will church growth methodology help us here, or does it further encourage us to desert the city? Can it be that the image of "gathering and scattering" as people in transit is more consistent with the people of God concept than is the picture of a steepled white clapboard building in the heart of the village green? Can it be that the tabernacle is a better visual representation of the people of God than is the temple? Must we judge success in terms of building cathedrals and gathering the largest media constituency? Can the church succeed in our kind of time only if the pastor is viewed as the dominating kingly figure, or is it appropriate to be pilgrims together, with direction and discipleship shared by the nonclergy? Does the congregational form of church government facilitate mission, or does it impede any form of church growth in the contemporary world?

Although there is biblical clarity that the church was never called into being primarily for herself, it is equally clear that the church as an institution, in her necessity for self-preservation, often loses the essence of the church as mission and violates the very life to which she is called as the people of God. I am committed to the church as an institution and believe that every organism must have some organized, institutional form. I remain part of her from a reflective position of intentionality. I know her disease and her promise. Yet as I contemplate the church today, and from where I serve as the senior pastor of a church in the city, I would judge that the church as an institution is in serious trouble, and every main-line denomination is faced with the same agonies.

I have great ambiguities as to what to do about this trouble. Part of those ambiguities are born from the fact that I have very conservative roots. Much of the value system which remains with me came from those roots, and I am grateful to those who contributed to this value system and grateful that certain aspects of it have continued with me along the way. I desperately need some help. Can the church growth movement provide some of that help? Will it honor that which is conservative within me and at the same time allow enough freedom to honor the more liberal branches that experience has caused to sprout from those roots and has nurtured across the years?

An even deeper question gnaws within. Is it possible to ''be the church'' and be a successful institution at the same time? I look at the ''religious variety shows,'' which are certainly successful at ''packing them in,'' and wonder whether this has much to do with the church. I read the literature of the leaders of these ''successful churches'' and learn the basic thesis that one should never, never say anything unpleasant. I hear the encouragement to eschew any prophetic stance and always send people away feeling good.[2] All of the voices of the prophets contest, and the calls to counterculture cry within me. My absentee mentor, Dietrich Bonhoeffer, comes back and reminds me that there is no ''cheap grace.'' Must it be— as the Jerry Falwells, Pat Robertsons, and Rex Humbards claim—that they are destined to be the ''fishers of men'' and the remainder of us have a decreasing assignment as ''keepers of the aquarium''?

Shall I continue to view the church as at its best when it contradicts the natural groupings of human beings, when it contradicts the idea that the church in order to be authentic must be heterogeneous, reconciling the educated and uneducated, the black and the white, the high and the low? Or is the church better, or at least more successful, when it conforms to such groupings? Should the church accommodate itself to social and caste systems, or is the church, as Liston Pope suggested, called to be *The Kingdom Beyond Caste*? Is Gibson Winter's *The Suburban Captivity of the Churches* something to be blessed and fostered if it contributes to numerical success, or is that very captivity a violation of the church?

I suppose I am even asking whether it is possible to ''be the church'' and be a successful institution at the same time. Those surely at times do coincide, but is building a successful institution to be my primary goal? I would judge that a numerically declining institution is no evidence of a true church, but can it be true that at times such is the correlation?

The Outward Look

Another question calls: Is it legitimate to center primary attention upon the inward concerns of building a successful institution when the biblical people of God are ever called to an outward journey? The voices of dispossessed and disenfranchised people cry mightily. Growth has been the secular religion of American society. The maximization of self-interest in "being successful" has been a driving force. The church has blessed multinational corporations in the name of success. Do we now listen to the voices of liberation theologians, condemn the roots of wealth planted deep in the misery of the Third World,[3] and thus endanger our own success? Do we recognize that biblical religion in both Testaments is concerned about the little people of the earth, or shall we minimize this because it makes people uncomfortable and they can find more positive thinking at the church-store around the corner? Are we to leave these questions untouched and hope that *after* we get the increasing numbers into the church, *then* some conversions may take place and some attention will be given to the needs?

All of these are questions that impinge on the nature of the church. They are questions that the church growth movement relates to in one way or another. We do need to keep the institution together. We do need to be successful; yet at the same time we need to be faithful to what we believe the church to be. Furthermore, is the church growth movement so theologically right-wing as to be uncomfortable even if its techniques work? Which way do we go? What do we do?

2

An Analysis of Church Growth in Light of a Theological Understanding of the Church

There is a growing body of church growth literature. Much of it has been motivated by the work of the School of World Mission and Institute of Church Growth at Fuller Theological Seminary. My impression from reading the church growth books is that people interested in the field are becoming more sophisticated and increasingly using better sources and resources in authenticating their concern. The circle of interested participants is being extended beyond fundamentalistic conservatives to touch all varieties of theological camps and persuasions. Although credit for the emphasis, much needed in the contemporary church, must be given to the technicians of church growth, one gains the distinct impression that the further removed the participants are from the technicians, the less dogmatic is the style and the more compatability there is with moderate and liberal Christians. The question, of course, is whether the positives outweigh the negatives.

The Positive Spirit

Daring to believe is the biggest thing church growth people have going for them. Sometimes their believing almost reaches the proportions of the little red engine puffing up the hill, saying, "Yes, I can, yes, I can, yes, I can." But at least they do not manifest a depressed and defeatist mentality, passively sitting in the corner, hiding within the fortress, and using all of their energy just to "hold on" as is true of so many main-line churches. The church growth people are certainly interested in multiplying themselves; they believe they can multiply themselves, and they feel a mandate to do so. They sense a mandate to conversion. The first thing one must do in a critique of church growth efforts is to accept or reject that mandate. As one does so, he or she must recognize that the *principle* of growth and the techniques of growth are two different things.

At this moment, we are dealing with the principle of growth, and growth is perceived as a matter of attitude. Growth is a matter of attitude; it is a style, a way of life for the church, the pastor, and each individual. In fostering that attitude, it is suggested that "church growth is a way of thinking, planning, and doing. It is not a program that is conducted once or twice per year. It is a way of life for the church." [1] Growth is a matter of conscience and relates to the belief that churches can have what they want if they "will do the right things." [2] It is that "do-the-right-things" concept that so distressingly bothers many of us. Consideration must be given to it at a later point in our discussion. The emphasis does, however, undergird the intensity of the attitude.

The possibility of growth is accompanied by the desire to grow. According to C. Peter Wagner, "The indispensable condition for a growing church is that it wants to grow." [3] This desire is accompanied by a sense of expectancy. Church growth people live with the attitude of William Carey, founder of the modern missionary movement, who stressed that if you expect great things from God, you will receive great things from God. Isaiah's lengthening of cords and strengthening of stakes are part of the very consciousness of church growth people (Isaiah 54:2). This sense of expectancy enables them to give rebuttal to despair. As McGavran suggests,

> But, of course, someone will say, "Wait a minute. These people are utterly indifferent to the church." My answer to that is that the indifference may be in *us* rather than in *them*. If we believe that these people are not going to be interested, then perhaps *for us* they won't be! But they are basically receptive. Again and again, around the world, as I have studied the growth of the church, I find communities where some new church, some new denomination, even some new person coming in, finds a responsiveness that the older group didn't find. I can only conclude that the responsiveness was there all along. [4]

This sense of expectancy is based on what Charles Mylander calls the "four mandates": the great commission, the great commandment, the great commitment, and the great concern. [5] Church growth people take the so-called "great commission" of Matthew's Gospel (28:18-20) quite literally, indeed as they do most of the Bible. Armed with the Great Commission, they will not listen to the "God-can't-do-that-here syndrome." [6] What Robert Schuller categorizes as "impossibility thinking" [7] is not allowed, for such unbelief expresses itself in an unwillingness to risk. [8] This, again, is the attitude of believing that it can be done and then setting out to do what appears to be the impossible. We are reminded that "the faith dimension of the work of God does not come into focus until a church extends herself beyond her resources."[9] The attitude of belief is fostered by constant self-study and motivational therapy, which is designed to eradicate any doubtful tendencies, for "when people are wedded to a conclusion, there develops a state of mind which makes them blind to evidence that does not support the conclusion."[10]

In a rather simplistic way church growth people place their growth success all upon human shoulders and negate the reasons sometimes listed for not growing and call those reasons "nothing more than rationalizations built on decades of stagnation."[11] Although many of us who work in transient urban areas would struggle with such simplistic and categorical statements, it is hard to deny that mental attitudes play a big part in the failure to bear fruit.

Over and over again the thesis is propounded that if churches are healthy, they *will* grow. If they are not healthy, they will not grow. Categorically growth is a sign of health. In every instance non-growth is viewed as an evidence of death and sickness. It is particularly in evaluating this part of the attitudinal stance that one must have some inherent understanding as to the nature of the church. There will no doubt be great debate as to what constitutes "health." One gets the impression from reading the literature that if you do not have health, then, like a mechanic, you do some tinkering until you get what can be described as health, i.e., an increase in numbers. This "increase in health" may be attached to religious variety shows, contests, or almost anything. A positive attitude is one thing, but Mylander's statement is a bit much when he suggests that after reading books by McGavran and his associates in church growth and attending a church-growth seminar, "I returned and made a couple of changes, and our church began to grow."[12] If the tinkering according to instructions does not do it, you are left to believe that you are working in an unproductive place; the next step is to cease "casting pearls before swine" and to move to a "healthier" location which effectively deserts urban life and urban people and moves to succeeding concentric suburban rings of the city. This utilitarian attitude turns a positive attitudinal stance into the negative, all motivated by the adage that every church should grow; every church can grow.[13]

Some might wish to suggest that the growth attitude is both desirable and legitimate but that there is a difference between qualitative growth and quantitative growth and that one may be appropriate for one place and the other for another. It is the contention of church growth adherents, however, that qualitative growth always produces quantitative growth, for "quality that does not produce quantity is counterfeit."[14] One appreciates the corollary that is quickly added, which also holds that "quantitative growth that does not end in qualitative growth will disappear."[15] Although not all church growth specialists hold such a positive attitude, an increasing number do. It is the judgment of this writer, however, that the institute at Fuller has cranked out such a promotion program for its materials that the quality aspects are not nearly as important as counting the numbers. Attention will be given later to the discipling aspects of church growth as related to the qualitative concept.

Kinds of Growth

At this point, however, since the kinds of growth are so closely related to the attitudinal stance, some attention must be given to them. Following the lead of McGavran, all of the proponents speak of four kinds of growth: internal growth, expansion growth, extension growth, and bridging growth. Most of the attention in the literature is given to expansion growth.

Chaney and Lewis have a more balanced concern and make it clear that "growth includes reproduction as well as increasing weight and size."[16] Thus, they give much support to internal growth, namely, the spiritual nurture of those who are already members of a local congregation. They recognize that the Christian life is a pilgrimage and that we are ever journeying towards wholeness and maturity. Small groups, Bible study, prayer fellowships, and a whole host of other possibilities are part of the internal growth pattern. This emphasis is appreciated very much. It is disturbing, however, to find a certain arrogance in some of the material which suggests that internal growth is necessary because of the assumption that vast armies of church people are unregenerated and need a conversion experience that is defined in a particular way.[17] It is this "looking down the nose" sense of expressed superiority, occurring with such frequency within the literature, which would turn off some inquirers.

Of course, the primary concern within the literature is expansion growth—finding more members and adding them to the local church. It is fair to say that not all church growth adherents have the same interest in "adding them to the local church." Many of the electronic church people seem to be more concerned with adding them to their mailing lists for financial purposes. Nevertheless, the principle of expansion is the same. Expansion growth anticipates that 10 percent of the church leadership will commit itself to a priority and continuous effort to go beyond the walls of the church building and reach those who are unchurched. Expansion growth anticipates some growth by the biological process, and it actively seeks transfer possibilities; but the primary focus is in conversion growth. In these times of zero population growth and a singles constituency in many churches, there must be an alert awareness that for a church to rely on biological growth is for that church slowly to commit suicide.[18]

A third form of growth is extension growth, which primarily means planting new churches. The church growth people believe that this area has been sadly neglected and suggest that any denomination in America could reverse its membership decline by developing an aggressive extension growth program.[19] The technicians suggest that presently there are only half enough churches in the United States.[20] To many of us who always seem to labor in overchurched areas, such an idea seems preposterous. Support for the need for more churches comes from statistics from the Glennary Research Center, which reports that there are eight states that show that fifty percent or more of their population are without church affiliation.[21] Southern Baptists have been particularly successful in extension growth. Their thesis is that any church will do better if it has two meeting places rather than one. In citing examples, Chaney and Lewis appear to suggest that this becomes a means of phasing out one location where returns are diminishing and being prepared to do all of the business in the new shop where larger numbers are a possibility.[22] Although one is attracted to the idea of "chapel" locations, I am not attracted to the underlying thesis in church growth that God calls always to the more successful locations. Urban life will ultimately be forsaken of witness if this thesis is followed. The method is highly recommended as a much more "cost-effective" way to do evangelism.[23]

Bridging growth is the last of the four forms of church growth. This is planting churches across cultural lines in areas where the people are not "our kind of people." Whereas this has been a practice in so-called "foreign missions," it now means being intentional about a Chinese or Japanese community or section of the city. Church growth adherents contend that 84 percent of the world's population must be won this way.[24] Although this approach sounds most reasonable for many places in the world, it offers little help for a church already located in a community that is culturally diverse. Cultures increasingly are not neatly scattered and separated. Can it be that the church simply cannot minister and succeed in a community of diversity?

All of the above definitions assume that we will sow only where there is likely to be the most success. Planning for each of these kinds of growth will take into account the same procedures that McDonald's restaurant chain uses in determining where to locate its next unit.

The Great Commission

But each of the previous definitions is also based on the assumption that Matthew 28:18-20 is taken very seriously and that it is a mandate to witness. Here, with due credit to the advocates, we are looking at the rationale and the motivation behind the streamlined techniques. It is significant that the incident we have come to know as "the Great Commission" immediately follows the narrative of the resurrection. This *may* be the first public gathering after the resurrection when other than the apostles—namely, the five hundred referred to by Paul in 1 Corinthians 15—were present. The very first message for these gathered disciples is that there is a world waiting out there.

This basic biblical beginning is a call to remember that "the church exists by mission as a fire exists for burning" and church growth people take that very seriously. When mission is lost, church existence loses its vitality. Mission is thus viewed not as a sideline but as the lifeline of the church. Who can or who wants to disagree with this thesis? We may disagree about its full meaning, and it will be argued later in another place that the full social dimensions of this mandate are not grasped by the technicians. Indeed, they are frightened by the social dimensions. Nevertheless, churches in the main-line and more liberal traditions have been asleep here. Recently when a minimal suggestion was made from my own pulpit that "everyone win one," there was a great deal of surprise expressed, as though this were most unusual and certainly highly unlikely. Such a sharing of the faith on a one-on-one basis may always have been inherent in the church's mission, but it is not a pattern for much of contemporary Christianity.

The church growth adherents have demonstrated rather convincingly that when any church omits a missionary program of some sort as primary in its activity, the result is tragic. The people lose their vision and become narrow-minded. They lose their concern and become self-centered. When we lose our imperative concern for the world that is waiting out there, we soon die spiritually. The "world" is defined as anyone outside the church and, in theory, the concern is about every individual from where one lives to the outer limits of humankind. In terms of practice, however, church growth people migrate to the most likely assured success spots for the place to pursue this mission.

The previously discussed attitude of expectancy is tied to the interpretation of the phrase that recognizes a participal form as laying out the expectation for the church. It is not merely "go into all the world . . ." but rather "as you are going. . . ." It is just natural and normal that you will go. A sense of triumph is connected with the movement. If the purpose is to share the Good News and the place to do it is the whole world, then the power to get it done is rooted in a human obedience that recognizes that one does not work alone. A divine traveling companion is promised. "I am with you always until the end of the age" assures that the mission is not just a human enterprise. Church growth people work, however, as though outreach is a human enterprise and that the success depends on the right human engineering at precisely the right time. Any biblical and theological assessment would wish to call us back to the resurrection of Jesus Christ as both the declaration and proof of authority. Without it that earliest little band of disillusioned disciples would hardly have stirred to win the world, and without it present disciples can hardly do so. Add to this the great conviction of conservative Christians that Christ is the saving Redeemer who makes a difference and ferment within church growth activity is assured.

The Great Commission is translated into a mandate for the particular strategies of the McGavran group:

> Church Growth is directly related to God's will. God wants his church to grow. The Lord Jesus, on the occasion of his last appearance to the apostles, said, "All authority in heaven and on earth has been given to me. Go therefore and make disciples" (Matt. 28:18, 19, RSV). It's just as plain as that. Any church not concerned with growth and discipleship is really disobeying God and is doing what is *not* pleasing to him. His express will is that the good news of the gospel be communicated to all people, all classes, all races, and all languages near and far, geographically and culturally.[25]

It may not have been intentional that "Growth" is capitalized in the preceding quote, but it is, and does lead one to feel that the Institute people in California thus understand their program to be *the* one which is best an extension of the Commission. But the enthusiasm for the Commission is there, and it is understood as still set in our time and will not allow us to forget those 150,000,000 Americans whom McGavran and Arn declare to be "either pagans or marginal Christians who not only *need* to be but *can* be discipled,"[26] with some of these persons living around every church.

With the Great Commission as their context, McGavran and Arn list what they call "biblical principles" of church growth. Their literal approach to the Scriptures is disconcerting to one who understands the nature of the biblical revelation in a more dynamic way. Those who differ from their understanding of the infallibility and authority of Scripture are perceived as having a "low view of the authority of the Scriptures."[27] Nevertheless, the connection of their "biblical principles" with the Commission is clear. They understand that outsiders, those people without Jesus Christ, are *really lost,* and yet they are quite sure that God's love and concern are for all people. Christ is viewed as the *one* way, the only way, and the Holy Spirit, who inspired Christ's early people, will walk through our lives today and give power for growth. In order to carry out the Commission, it is, therefore, necessary to spend more time praying specifically for the growth of the church. They want us to spend more time specifically praying for the conversion of people—friends and loved ones—rather than spending so much time praying for the infirmities of the body. They characterize our present prayer meetings as sounding more like "infirmary roll calls." Although at some point we will want to scrutinize the call to benign neglect of the already churched, the focus upon the unchurched is directly connected to the mandate to be found in the Great Commission.[28]

Added to the Great Commission are all of the many figures that express the same theme in another way—harvest, the catch of fish, the notion of inheritance. These figures likewise denote expectancy and suggest that we have the task of ingathering, mandating that we go after the "unpossessed possessions" lest we as human agents be part of the actual obstruction of God's work.[29]

Hindrances to Growth

With such expectancy and positive thrust, what can possibly be the hindrances to growth?

According to church growth persons, the introverted congregation is probably the largest single deterrent to growth. This preoccupation with "our own congregation" consumes the time of pastor as well as people. I certainly must admit this as I reflect on my own experience. Every person and every family has a story. They need all of the help they can get in taking care of the wounds that they experience. When you finish taking care of one wound, there is another awaiting attention. It is not that an aggressive distress signal is sent out. It is that the pastor develops that "sixth" sense and seeks out those whose pattern changes or who are missing. Those of the laity are busy enjoying one another. I am part of a wonderful church with a very rich fellowship where people enjoy one another. It has occurred to me, however, that there are very few "entrance points" for newcomers. It is a great fellowship if you are already in, but it is difficult to find the point of entry. I discover also that if there are six parishioners who are ill and six nonmember prospects, I always take care of the parishioners first and maybe get to the six nonmembers within the next two or three weeks. Church growth people have provided a valuable service in calling attention to the internal preoccupation. At the same time, people in the movement are so anxious to grow that their priorities almost suggest that one be pastorally unconcerned about those already in the fold.

A similar hindrance to church growth is the tendency to be chained to nonproductive work.[30] Meetings, administrative tasks, and unplanned agendas can consume an inordinate amount of time. "Tending the store" must be replaced by vigorous outreach.[31] That our vision is blinded by domestic and denominational tending the store and housekeeping is without a doubt true.

Throughout the growth material, there is a constant challenge to measure and to engage in what is called "growth accounting." Many congregations do not know the reality of their situations. Busy activities may hide the fact that decline has set in. Businesses constantly do an inventory to reflect the state of health. The failure of churches to do so impedes the motivation to growth. The pastor is the key person in getting this done. He generally is aware of the numerical statistics but may find it difficult to get them out into the open lest they reflect his or her own sense of failure and because he or she hesitates to have these statistics used as a yardstick of his or her work. Church units of nearly every denomination compile some kind of annual report for their denominational offices. These "membership audits" need to be used to motivate us to a serious analysis of the local situation and in the development of programs of outreach. In the use of statistics, however, it is important to keep the motivation straight. In all of the church growth literature, the only caution I found against "the success-at-all-costs syndrome prevalent in today's society" was in Chaney and Lewis.[32] Many of us have had the experience of seeing new people in terms of what they can mean in the maintenance of the institution. A couple of days before this writing an individual joined our church and a lay member said to me, "He can mean a lot to us because he is a good giver." He was thinking in terms of the church budget, of course. But this thinking is not peculiar to lay persons. Many is the time I have struggled with keeping pure the focus of my own motivation. This temptation to emphasize what the "individual can mean to us" rather than relating to the person from a genuine caring and serving concern is easily pervasive. In the struggles of institutional life, one finds oneself questioning why one should spend so much time bringing pastoral support to that individual who "can contribute nothing." Membership auditing and the appropriate use of the statistics is vital to motivation for growth, but at the same time let us strive for integrity of concern and the refusal to evaluate people on the basis of "what they can mean to us."

Another hindrance to growth is in limiting the scope of concern only to those who like things and do things "just like us." This was certainly a large measure of the basic conflict that necessitated the Jerusalem Conference in Acts 15. The Jerusalem church was insisting that Gentile Christianity be a duplicate of its own Hebrew background and culture. All of us who work in centers of great urban mix know how difficult it is to challenge successfully the older Anglo nucleus to open its interest to the new people within the community. The same people who find it exciting to send mission dollars overseas to "win the foreigners" find it very difficult to have a sense of openness when those same people move next door. This attitude is not, however, confined to urban communities. Years ago when I was a student pastor in a rural location where there was an influx of migrant workers each summer, I made the "mistake" of facilitating their attendance at our little country church. The hew and cry from the regulars was, "They are not our kind of people."

But there is great ambivalence in the church growth material about this. We are warned against limiting our focus to one group of people, and statistics are used to support the counsel. Although I do not like the term "melted" as reflecting a melting pot syndrome in which everyone is "melted down" into some homogenized mix, it is concluded from studies that only 56.6 percent of our population is "melted" and that we must go after that 43.4 percent—and increasing—unmelted group.[33] This hindrance of limiting concern to one segment of the population at the same time carries with it a recognition of how difficult it is to cross the barriers of culture, language, education, wealth, employment, etc. Whereas we, at points in the church growth literature, are faced with the danger of addressing ourselves only to "our own kind," much of the remainder of the literature is concerned with the difficulty of crossing those barriers. As a result, the homogeneous principle is developed around the thesis that every individual should be able to become a Christian with his or her own kind of people and should not have to cross any of these barriers. A new separatism is promoted which inevitably will become self-defeating again and close the doors to those who are "not like us." The homogeneous principle, the backbone of church growth strategy, will be discussed in a later section dealing with negative factors in the church growth program. It will suffice here to say that there is great ambiguity in that what is pushed as a hindrance to growth is at the same time portrayed as one of the major strategies for growth.

Another hindrance is our blindness to the people who are right around us. Why is it that so many of us will drive miles and miles across the city to visit a prospect but do not know who lives behind the doors across the street from our church buildings? To be sure, it is easier to "go after" the person who on his or her own has first sought us out by visiting a worship service. There is something, however, that often leads us to assume that the people closest to us are not interested. It is sad but true that we often do not know our community—its residents, its institutions, its traditions, its changing nature. It is a rather natural assumption that those right around us are of some religious or denominational persuasion unlike our own and, therefore, are not interested. However, we do not live in a period of extreme denominational loyalty. If they are unchurched, with some exceptions to be sure, they are just as likely prospects for our church in their neighborhood as they are for a church of their original denomination located some distance away. In any city, less than 20 percent are in any church on any given Sunday, but the focus of concern should be upon those within a five- to ten-mile radius.[34] Sometimes this not knowing the people about us is related to our psychological depression as to the possibility of interesting people in the cause of Christ and the church. Hope and expectancy are hallmarks of growth. If we truly know our community and its people, we will find a need and fill it.

Another detriment to growth is the church's surrender of its distinctive character. In trying to appeal to a pluralistic society, we have become too much like it. Someone suggested that the church is like the chameleon which died from exhaustion in crossing a piece of scotch plaid. What is true for the church as a whole is certainly true for the individual members. When the Christian community loses its distinctive style and value system, its peculiar character and priority to a holy God who requires holy obedience, it can hardly be attractive to others. Certainly we do not desire a superficial and hypocritical arrogance, but it would appear that the unchurched community expects something of us, and when we do not deliver, their disappointment drives them to become more removed in interest. There was a time when we majored in "preaching at" our community. In more recent years, even when we have come to know our community, we have developed social and other outreach ministries of presence without sharing the distinctive flavoring of the proclamation that makes possible true humanness. I would not want his suggestion to become a cop-out for avoiding the social thrust of the Christian gospel, but we do need to hear Alan Tippett's reminder that "we cannot offer a service demonstration as a substitute for gospel proclamation."[35] I do not desire to mark an extreme difference between "evangelizing the world" and "Christians seeking to make the world a better place," as does McGavran, but the balance of interest is important. I would hasten to add that there are times when "making the world a better place" is evangelism.

But perhaps the greatest hindrance of all is that we just are not willing to take the risks and make the investments that growth requires. It does cost time and money and a high investment of energies. But when this is accompanied by goals, then the goals are in some sense a statement of faith.[36] Although the development of quality programs is most important, this can never take the place of projected goals, which give a plan of mobilization and action. Urban churches of the downtown type often speak of offering the kind and quality of music and activity that others cannot offer as a means of attracting people. Although this, of course, helps, it is not sufficient. People respond to the personal contact and warmth of other people who are motivated by high purpose. Until we get them there, the program is not very beneficial.

It is time to end this section and to conclude it as it began. Church growth people believe that the greatest hindrance of all to growth is in simply not believing and not risking. The adherents of church growth are absolutely convinced that their methodology and their purpose are somehow part of a divine plan. They claim much for themselves and their plan when they evaluate it as being "very close to the unswerving purpose of God."[37] This commitment creates an optimism in which they expect great advance in the church, certainly a different spirit than that in the main-line church where we are often defeated and near despair. Main-line people are beginning to pick up the spirit. George G. Hunter, Secretary of Evangelism for the United Methodist Board of Discipleship, has written an excellent volume on evangelism with a foreword by Donald McGavran of church growth fame. Calling his volume *The Contagious Congregation,* he writes: "I believe that mainline Protestant Christianity, although declining today, can and will once again become a contagious movement among the people of

North America."[38] He is convinced that if we learn how to offer what we truly have to offer, there will be a major surge of faith and response. Expectancy and risk are the challenge: "It is better by noble boldness to risk being subject to half the evils we anticipate than to remain in cowardly listlessness for fear of what may happen."[39]

When this sense of expectancy is accompanied by a high sense of morale built from satisfying experiences and from a sense of unselfishness that both looks outwardly and releases its money for outward mission concerns, a church character is developed that helps attract others. Mylander quotes some research that indicates that those churches giving 19 to 25 percent of their funds to outside causes have a better numerical growth record than do those churches that primarily are involved in spending their money to pay for buildings, salaries, supplies, and other internal needs.[40] This conclusion may be based on data which is too limited, however. In the heated debates on the biblical inerrancy questions which are taking place in the Southern Baptist Convention, it is my understanding that those who classify themselves as moderates are waging a campaign to recapture leadership of the Convention (the presidency and other offices) and that they are doing so on the thesis that the very conservative churches do not very well support outside causes, meaning by that, the Cooperative Program (mission program arm) of Southern Baptists. Many of the rapidly expanding churches do appear to be very conservative and are involved in huge building programs that require enormous sums to be spent at the home base. This may indicate a temporary situation until the huge real estate holdings are paid for, but in any case, the same sense of expectancy and enthusiasm is there in both cases. It almost sounds as if "stirring up the pot and beating the drums" is more important than is any substance delivered once the attention of the masses has been captured. One hopes this is not the case.

Characteristics of Growing Churches

All of the writers in the church growth movement appear to have near consensus on what might be called the characteristics of growing churches. Although they may differ in exact number from writer to writer, the numerical difference is primarily a matter of difference in classification. These characteristics are summarized and classified here and in some instances will be evaluated in a later section where the negatives of church growth are discussed.

Growth Goal Consciousness

There is unanimity among advocates of church growth, as stressed earlier, that you must develop a growth goal consciousness; you must sustain a growth atmosphere that projects one goal after another. Chaney and Lewis reflect the outlook of most of the material in suggesting that a growth atmosphere is one in which things are always pleasant and painless. This atmosphere is designed to focus on the comforts and life needs of the individual and is supported by things which make it easy for the participants, such as modern nurseries and larger-than-needed parking lots and all of the good things that might draw people to a shopping center rather than to the traditional downtown area. Ministry is directed primarily to where people hurt and caters to the personal desires of the individual. In Robert Schuller's case this means the outlawing of any focus upon "sin," for sin is a negative thought and something about which people do not like to think. Growth atmospheres are connected to "possibility thinking," which Chaney and Lewis translate to mean that "growing churches respect the wants and needs of those they are reaching or trying to reach. A church that wants to grow must make the first-time attendance experience as pleasant as possible."[41]

Such a growth-conscious atmosphere is designed to provide a service impression rather than a challenge impression. Participation in the religious life is made as easy as possible. You know whom you are trying to impress, and you design things that way.[42] The goals are always goals calculated to produce growth. There is no motivation in a "no goals" atmosphere, and a "maintenance goal" only invites self-defeatism and despair. This growth consciousness that majors in putting people at ease and creates its design primarily to service those who are invited in must be evaluated. It is a proven technique, however, in building a successful institution. A problem-centered approach does not work, but to "find a need and fill it" will.[43]

The Use of the Laity

I want to note a difference between "the use of laity" and "the ministry of laity" and suggest that the church growth emphasis is more on the "use" of laity. Church growth people sometimes seem to be indicating that a strong pastor must be master of the church situation. Nevertheless, there is a recognition in all of their literature that laity must be mobilized, involved, and trained and that growth is impossible unless there is a recognition that all of the members of the congregation are the ministers of the church. The pastor will work diligently to enable the lay people to prepare themselves to accomplish their ministry.

Church leaders are divided into categories, or "classes."

CLASS I leaders concern themselves primarily with the maintenance of what the church is as it presently exists. These are the people who staff the institutional life and do all of those things necessary to keep the organization together. They are our trustees, Sunday school teachers, choir members, and other laity who selflessly give of themselves from a strong sense of loyalty. People should not forever remain in this category. They grow stale and lose a sense of vision. Often they become protective of "what is."

It is wholesome, therefore, for Class I leaders to become recruits for that group of lay people who are volunteers away from the church.

CLASS II. Many have gifts that are not needed for mere maintenance. These are the people who have a strong desire for outreach and have the drive and courage to touch base with the unchurched. Whereas Class I leaders are usually concerned with the people already on hand, Class II leaders are looking for new people to invite into the church and into a personal relationship with Jesus Christ. Others who belong in this category are those "community outreach" people who project the social thrust of the church and provide a ministry of "presence." However, the church growth movement gives little value to the "presence" kind of ministries and thinks more in terms of an active invitation of the unchurched to come to the church for salvation and security. Lay volunteers are the backbone of this movement. Sometimes Class I leaders are those in the church who are interested in qualitative growth. Class II people may have qualitative concerns, but their primary interest is upon quantitative growth. Classes I and II are primarily the unpaid people who carry on church life. They are in liaison with three additional categories.

CLASS III people are the paid and unpaid pastors of small churches, study groups, and evangelistic cells. Many of these "pastors" are lay people who feel called of God to function in this special way.

CLASS IV is comprised of the professional church leadership, ordained and unordained. These leaders have a special responsibility to equip and motivate the constituency of Classes I and II. It is especially important that these people be able to motivate and train those in Classes I and II. If this is an able group, it can be instrumental in enabling the other part of the church (99 percent) to look outward in its concerns.

CLASS V includes those paid functionaries who work primarily outside of the local church: denominational leaders, missionaries, professional teachers, etc.

It can readily be seen that the "shoulder to the wheel" work of the church is done by Classes I and II. If we survey the local situation, we will discover that routinely we use far more of our people in maintenance than in outreach. Mylander is surely correct in suggesting that "fifty times as many hours go into serving the saints as into evangelizing the neighborhood."[44]

Church growth people clearly view the Class II people as being the firing line kind of people through whom the church succeeds or fails. Although it is felt that not enough people fall into this category, the technicians suggest that only 10 percent of our total church members is needed to keep the church in an active growth state. It is, of course, important that many of these have the true gift of evangelism, which is the primary focus of the church growth movement. The people who commit themselves to Class II need a strong desire to share their faith with others. According to C. Peter Wagner, there is evidence to indicate that "if a church has 10 percent, or even a few percentage points less than 10 percent, of its active members mobilized for evangelism, a growth pattern of 200 percent per decade is a realistic expectation."[45] Wagner is not satisfied with the 10 percent figure, however. His recommendation is that we have a goal of 40 percent of church members in Class I and 20 percent as Class II workers.[46] Of these 20 percent, 10 percent will give themselves to door-to-door evangelism.

Although this is not the place for detailed appraisal, I must suggest that while I heartily agree with the dependence upon laity, it hardly seems plausible to expect 10 percent of them to be engaged in door-to-door evangelism, especially in the city. In areas of single-family residential units it might be possible, but in urban complexes of apartments and condominiums, it hardly seems likely. Security precautions make random door-to-door visitation an impossibility in urban areas. Furthermore, urbanites often do not exist in nuclear family units, and one seldom finds people at home without appointments. But then this lack of sensitivity to the city and focus upon the suburb is a problem in much of the church growth focus.

How will the laity be used? Orlando E. Costas suggests that the process of the mobilization of our laity requires four aspects: to motivate, to recruit, to organize, and to supervise.[47] These four involve a process of "conscientization" in which the people of God (in this instance, primarily the laity) develop an evangelistic conscience. In the process the congregation moves from a passive role, from being mere "gap fillers," to assume status as God's agents of mission. The pastor and professional leaders are viewed as resources.[48] These resources will help the laity in the process of analysis, planning, and evaluation. As the process develops, the laity will understand the church to have a double role:

> (1) that of a community being *brought together* by the Holy Spirit and the Word for empowering, instruction, analysis and planning; and (2) that of a team being *sent* into the world *to learn* how to serve the world, *to bear witness* for Christ by word and deed, *to be redemptively present* in the struggles of the world and *to call people* to enter the kingdom of God.[49]

Church growth people have even calculated how many resource people it will take to do the things mentioned here. Documented research is claimed for the suggestion that every 200 people must be led by a pastor and a support person (secretary). This recommendation is based on a computer analysis of the experience of 9,000 churches. The process of nurturing and training these lay people calls for groupings of ten Sunday school classes for every full-time minister.[50]

A Priority for Direct and Effective Evangelism

Growing churches are committed to evangelism.

George G. Hunter III utilizes three definitions of evangelism to help us understand what this mass of enabled laity is to do.

Evangelism is first defined as "what WE do to help make the Christian faith, life, and mission a live option to undiscipled people, both outside and inside the congregation."[51] The major focus is upon those people who are not followers of Jesus Christ both within and outside of the church and the major purpose is to incorporate them in a meaningful way into the body of Christ. There are those within church memberships who have not responded to Christ as Messiah, and concern must be expressed for them. However, since 90 percent of our effort is already directed internally, deliberate attention will be directed externally. Hunter, more than any of the other people who have embraced the church growth movement, is very insistent that the goal is to press not only for decision but also for discipleship and incorporation into the body of believers. We take seriously the divine expectation that human beings are to be the ambassadors (2 Corinthians 5:20) who represent Christ in the presentation of this exciting opportunity.

But of course more than human effort is involved, for "evangelism is also what JESUS CHRIST does through the church's *kerygma* (message), *koinonia* (fellowship), and *diakonia* (service) to set people free."[52] Hunter places more emphasis on preaching than do some of the church growth adherents, and this will be discussed in our overall evaluation of the movement. It is within the contagious fellowship that the message of God's saving grace is sounded, and the message will be lived out in the service examples of those who share the message. These three methods of proclamation, fellowship, and service are effectively used only if God's Spirit is moving through the circumstances and events of the lives of those who need to be reached. This part of the definition of evangelism is a wholesome corrective to the overemphasis on "scientific technique" that permeates all of the materials coming from McGavran, Arn, and Wagner.

The third part of the definition is the conclusion that "evangelizing happens when the RECEIVER (receptor, respondent) turns (1) to Christ, (2) to the Christian message and ethic, (3) to a Christian congregation, and (4) to the world, in love and mission—*in any order*."[53] These four "turnings" represent far more depth of Christian understanding than is obvious in many other materials of the School of World Mission and Institute of Church Growth. All four turnings are necessary, or else the respondent will probably be one of the "problem" people discovered within nearly all congregations. These "turnings" are definitely aided by the wholeness inherent in part two of evangelism's definition, for "if it is by *kerygma* that the Christian faith is taught, and by *koinonia* that it is caught, then it is as a by-product of *diakonia* that the Christian faith is bought.!"[54]

McGavran and Arn summarize the nature of evangelism under two facets, "attraction" evangelism and "proclamation" (or "seek") evangelism.

While the quality of life on the part of believers needs to be such that others are attracted to Christ and the church, the limitations of this "unintentional evangelism" are explained. Remember that the church growth movement is interested in *growth,* and mere attraction evangelism does not accomplish much of that. The study of church budgets will indicate the minor amount of effort and attention given in many places to "seek" evangelism.[55]

McGavran insists that "equipping laity for ministry" is too general a phrase and that we must become more specific in challenging them and in training them for evangelism. Five qualities are needed: (1) biblical convictions about salvation, (2) a willingness to give regular time to evangelism, (3) basic training in evangelism, (4) that those involved regularly report to their sending body, and (5) prayer. It is suggested that if Christians have these qualities of leadership and if they are trained, then much of the fatigue resulting from a lack of success will disappear from our congregations.[56]

As for nearly everything else, church growth people have placed evangelism into a scheme in which there are four varieties: E-0, E-1, E-2, and E-3.

E-0 Evangelism (Evangelism Zero) primarily relates to winning nominal Christians, baptized unbelievers, and lapsed members to a more fervent commitment. Effort is directed toward the development of a more lively faith *within* the church. It is assumed in this kind of evangelism that one is working primarily within homogeneous groupings with few, if any, cultural, economic, or other kinds of barriers to cross. Within this kind of evangelism there is concentration upon winning the children of members, etc. Internal growth and biological growth are the foci. At the same time, it does appear to be assumed that the methods of church growth will sweep into the church many people whose lives have experienced no basic change so that their evangelization is necessary from within.

This is more sharply defined in E-1 Evangelism, which is addressed directly to "assimilated Americans who are confessed non-Christians."[57] Here again we are reaching out primarily to our "own kind of people" whom we find in the routine circles of our lives: relatives, business acquaintances, friends, club members and associates, etc. E-1 Evangelism is done within those familiar segments of society in which one has a specific identity and in which the people involved have such similarities that transfer to the church requires the crossing of few, if any, barriers.

E-2 Evangelism recognizes that there are people who must not only cross the barrier from non-Christian to Christian but who also have to cross racial, language, or socioeconomic barriers. E-2 Evangelism is focused on "culturally distinct Americans who are not believing, practicing Christians."[58] Attention in this form of evangelism is given to small groupings of people where a very friendly and comfortable small group or circle can be established, such as in a home fellowship. Proponents of church growth assume that not very many E-2 people can be assimilated into an already established church, and so the ultimate goal with these people is to establish new churches. According to the church growth view, one wants to be very careful lest the differences of culture are so great in a local church unit that the unit cannot cohere. Church growth people assume that a black family of the same basic cultural and economic status as the bulk of a church's white members may be included. However, a number of families different from the basic constituency or nucleus of the witnessing church, according to their review, require new units or an involvement in what church growth people call "bridging growth."

What begins to be a problem is definitely the focus in E-3 Evangelism. E-2 Evangelism creates culturally distinct churches, primarily within the United States. E-3 Evangelism is mostly concerned with world mission programs where the gaps or barriers to be crossed are both geographical and cultural, with no kinship in language, culture, or race.

Homogeneous Compatibility

The attention given to the kinds of evangelism necessitates discussion of *a* if not *the* primary characteristic claimed by church growth people for growing churches. It is also the characteristic with which I personally have the most difficulty and must evaluate in a later expression of negative response to the movement. I find it difficult to be fair in reporting this controlling philosophy but will attempt to be so.

The basic thesis of the church growth movement is that churches must be built with only homogeneous people. The "Bible" of church growth is still the primary work of Donald McGavran, *Understanding Church Growth*. He refers to homogeneity as "the sociological foundation" of his methodology. Over and over it is stressed through all of the literature that "men like to become Christians without crossing racial, linguistic, or class barriers."[59] The rationale is totally a practical one. A higher rate of conversion growth can be predicted for the homogeneous church. Therefore, it is important that a church be composed of basically one kind of people where people "feel at home" and know they are among "their kind of people." In spite of all of the aberrations of apartheid in South Africa, the "preference" of different dark-skinned peoples there to be in churches by themselves is used as illustrative material to substantiate the viewpoint. C. Peter Wagner even entitles one of his books *Our Kind of People* with the subtitle *The Ethical Dimensions of Church Growth in America*. Wagner devotes much attention to the "failure" of the social movements during the sixties and suggests that so it ought to be. In his section on creation in *Our Kind of People* he argues that since God made us this way, it is better to stay this way.[60]

Biblical justification for homogeneity is attempted. Genesis 11 is used in reverse. Church growth people say that God's intention was to keep the early peoples separated but they violated his wish by seeking to come together. Therefore, they were punished. John 4 is used to portray the separation between Jews and Samaritans, and this is viewed as proof that homogeneity is better.

The motivating factor is that the church must grow. Growth is the primary goal above everything else. Therefore, we are to remember that "birds of a feather flock together" and underscore as an *ought* that eleven o'clock on Sunday morning must remain a segregated hour. If there are any ethical, theological, and biblical dimensions that do not quite measure up to this supposition, these have to be evaluated in the light of what is believed to be God's higher desire for the church, that of growth.

In stressing the "separate but equal principle," church growth people propose thus to preserve the strengths of each group. In this advocacy of "cultural circumcision" (Wagner's term) it is argued that the strengths of all groups are best shared. These arguments are very much like the arguments that the Dutch Reformed church in tandem with the government of South Africa uses to champion apartheid.

Parallel to this emphasis on separatism, multi-individual and mutually independent decision making for the Christian cause is pushed as the norm. People do not easily become Christians individually. Therefore, things that emphasize separateness in the Christian life should be ignored and a "group comfort" should be developed. Since people have prejudices, these prejudices should be capitalized upon and made an aid to Christianity. A "tribal consciousness" should be developed in which you capture the main honchos and then get everyone else to sign on—a kind of group decision to become Christians. Tribes of people and homogeneous units of people are to develop the kinds of loyalties that give them a Christian consciousness in the same manner as was once possessed by the Scottish clans. We should become more conscious of sociological "people movements" and encourage people to become Christians through the "people movement" route. The one-by-one movement is not satisfactory because it is too hard to get people to go against the tide. Therefore, it is better to go with the tide.

Most opposition to the Christian movement, they believe, arises from sociological rather than from theological causes. Thus, using Jews as an example, they believe that if Jews could come to Christ without losing their identity as Jews, most of their theological difficulties would be greatly reduced. What would be wise would be the creation of a people's movement which was identified as Jewish, a kind of "Jews for Jesus," where people can have the best of both worlds. The idea is to make the Christian decision as easy as possible. The movement thus undertakes to examine the social and anthropological milieus in the midst of which churches multiply and show how knowledge of social structures aids in the recruitment of members.

Any social differences between people are perceived as strengths rather than weaknesses and are to be used as part of the social dynamics for ushering people into the church. Race consciousness is to be harnessed in such a positive way that Wagner can approve his mentor McGavran's statement: "It does no good to say that tribal peoples ought not to have race prejudice. They do have it and are proud of it. It can be understood and should be made an aid to Christianization."[61]

In attempting to justify the "our kind" viewpoint, Wagner turns to some big guns in the church struggle. He seeks to give rebuttal to the work of Jürgen Moltmann, for instance, who argues in *Religion, Revolution and the Future* that the church, to be authentic, must be heterogeneous, reconciling the educated and uneducated, the black and white, the high and the low. Moltmann sees the church at its best when it contradicts the natural groupings of human beings, and Wagner sees the church at its best when it conforms to such groupings. Wagner turns to the work of H. Richard Niebuhr, Liston Pope, and Gibson Winter and, appearing to reverse the intent of these people, uses their descriptions of the homogeneous disease as justification and defense for the homogeneous church. Niebuhr in *The Social Sources of Denominationalism* describes the principle of differentiation and therefore reaches negative conclusions about its justification. He pleads with us to overcome such divisions in his work *The Kingdom of God in America*. Gibson Winter in *The Suburban Captivity of the Churches* and Liston Pope in *The Kingdom Beyond Caste* decry the ethical degradation represented by such separateness and plead for correction. Wagner, on the other hand, takes their work as an indication of the way life is and seeks to use these works (based on a thesis totally opposite to his) to undergird the thesis that the church ought to accommodate itself to social and caste systems.[62]

The civil rights movement and the "black is beautiful" theme are both used as evidences that the separatist homogeneous principle is the correct one in growing churches; and besides, it works. Church ministry must always be done in a method, a manner, and a place where it succeeds. If it succeeds, it must be right. We must go only where people respond. According to church growth adherents, the early church allowed the numbers baptized to determine the focus of its mission so that "the New Testament Church went where men responded, believing this to be God's will."[63] We are cautioned "not to peer into ravines where there are no sheep."[64] In spite of what this appears theologically to say (a selective election based on the pragmatic principle), church growth people justify it in that in the long run more come into the kingdom this way. Justification is offered in that biblical parables emphasize not only the Lord's "seeking" but also his "finding" (lost coin, lost sheep, etc.), and so we must not waste time and effort on areas and persons where we cannot guarantee success.

Homogeneity more than anything else in the church growth thesis is viewed as a law. It is the platform of success, and if it has elements in it that appear to use the same reasoning as does the Dutch Reformed church and apartheid, it must be remembered that the defense is that such "consecrated pragmatism" works.

It has been difficult for me to report this part of the success formula. There is something deep within me which is severely pained at any plan that can view separatism as good. Nevertheless, I must wait until the appropriate opportunity in a later evaluation to share a personal critique.

Effort at Discipleship

A far more pleasant task is to report church growth's increasing emphasis on the necessity of discipleship as a criterion of success. It is most encouraging to find Win Arn calling for discipleship rather than mere decision making. His research indicated that there was often a "mortality rate of 75 percent among new converts." [65] Therefore, church growth has moved away from the isolated decision as a solo event to programs of sustenance through training in discipleship as a way of life and incorporation into the body of Christ. This movement from decision as a brief moment of time to the disciple emphasis as a lifelong task represents a definite maturing of the methodology. Orlando Costas continues to refine this aspect and challenges some of the earlier literature. He writes:

> Here lies a fundamental problem. The church has allowed itself to believe that making disciples is merely a quantitative task, *i.e.*, a numerical enterprise. It has assumed that the easier it makes it to follow Jesus, the more it adapts the gospel to the cultural situation, the more people will be able to be discipled. [66]

Dietrich Bonhoeffer's cry of "cheap grace," René Padilla's caution against "culture-Christianity" and Luis Segundo's description of "the massification of society" are all directed against any program which waters down the Christian life to a soft, comfortable way. The kind of discipleship is called for which would cause forty-nine Jesuit priests to risk the threat of death in order to stand by and alongside millions of landless and oppressed people in South America.

Admittedly this stringent call for discipleship, given as a characteristic of a growing church, is in contrast with much of the culture accommodation, which is used as the rationale for making it easier to win the masses. It may ultimately lead even to some refinement of the homogeneous principle. At the moment, however, it is in the infant stages of the church growth movement and is pursued because something must be done to avoid the 75 percent loss which Arn has discovered. Is church growth discovering that a church which "requires something" may ultimately be more successful than an invitation to a religious form of culture? Church growth nonetheless makes a much needed contribution in moving from a special crusade periodically to a consistent program fifty-two weeks per year. We applaud its stress that the Christian effort is not successful until it moves way beyond merely "buttonholing people for Jesus."

The emphasis upon small-group fellowships as a means of holding people and as a contribution to the maturation process is a decided improvement. Chaney and Lewis spell it out that "the principle of small groups is a basic principle of church growth."[67] Individual cells are essential for all living organisms. I discovered the validity of this principle when I became a member of Emmanuel Baptist Church in Albany, New York. A tired and depressed church began to show new life when Bible study and sermon discussion groups contributed both to the substantive nurturing of the people and to the building of individual units in which people discovered a sense of "belonging." These smaller units contributed to the dynamic of the corporate worship and the corporate worship in turn fed the smaller units.

A definite part of this discipling and small-group process is the renewed emphasis upon Bible study. It is exciting to have more and more churches making the discovery that Bible study is not just a Sunday school activity. Study of the Scriptures at other than Sunday school times and in other than church educational facilities (homes of members) may well release the study of the Bible from innocuous storytelling techniques to patterns of depth and struggle. We can be grateful to church growth for its focus on the Bible, both as a means of keeping people and of developing them into intellectually and emotionally growing people. It is encouraging that the new Bible study is more than a sharing of information by a teacher with pupils but rather a pursuit of the Bible in a context of fellowship with Christ and with one another.

At the same time that such Bible study is being promoted as a characteristic of the growing church, one does need to sound a caution. The approach to Bible study must be released from the literalistic, casebook-in-law kind of approach. Much of the rationale and defense of the church growth movement and methodology is based upon a literalistic, often out of context, approach to Scripture. One gets the impression that church growth continues to be geared to a propositional view of revelation. The Bible is not simply an answer book to which one addresses the proper question. What is revealed is not some *thing*. The revealer and the revealed are God. The Bible is a record of God's encounter with persons. The words can become the vehicle of a new revelation of that same God, the instrument of a new encounter. Bible study must grapple with the nature of that revelation and the nature of that God. A hermeneutic must be developed which aids one to discover what the message was then and how the *then* of that message gets translated into a valid principle now, and the bridge of that transfer must be sought. Exegesis, exposition, and application become a vital part of the process. The events of the past are not studied as history lessons but as events to be experienced. Both the student of and the record of those events come under the aegis of the Holy Spirit so that record plus Spirit may equal new revelation. The prolonged contribution of the Bible to the growth of the church will demand a more dynamic appreciation of the nature of the revelation. It demands the recognition that the Bible is not an "easy" book, and it demands the more determined preparation of people who are fit to lead and to teach.

An Appreciation of Gifts

Growing churches are based upon a recognition and appreciation of gifts, "spiritual gifts." I have always felt a bit squeamish about discussions of spiritual gifts. Few of the treatments of such biblical passages as Ephesians 4, Romans 12, and 1 Corinthians 12 have been helpful to me. Most of the treatments have little of substance about them. The search often appears to be directed to where nothing can be found, and much of the quest has related to ecstatic pursuits. But here we are speaking of gifts and church growth. Church growth brings its usual, practical results-producing eye to the question. And, of course, it does make sense that "it is counterproductive to chain people's energies in activities they are not gifted for."[68] The church far too long has operated on the army mentality of making cooks to be mechanics and mechanics to be cooks. I continue to be amazed that we take women and men and place them in church positions that seldom utilize the expertise that has made those same people successful in their profession or work. And who can but confess that if people served on the basis of their gifts rather than on the Peter principle (going from a level of competence to a level of incompetence, e.g., "homesteading" a church office), the church would be in much better shape?

I would not be so emphatic as to suggest that "ignorance of spiritual gifts may be a chief cause of retarded church growth today."[69] I would agree, however, that we must know who we are, corporately and individually (i.e., know our gifts), if we are to grow both numerically and qualitatively.

Wagner manages to find twenty-seven gifts. The list is long and perhaps labored and at times superficial, such as his discussion of the gift of hospitality and the ability to open one's home to visitors. Nevertheless, the overall contribution is real. It is helpful to reflect on the differentiation between "consecration theology" and "gift theology." One discovers the will of God through the examination of one's gifts. What we are called to do surely has some relationship to gifts, abilities, and interests.

The highlighting of gifts is an adjunct support to the emphasis on the role of laity in the life of the church, especially in the program of growth, and is another positive feature. It is most gratifying that attention is at least called to the vital place that women have in the life of the church. I have not been able to discern how the feminist cause might fare in the church growth emphasis. Little direct consideration is given, although there does seem to be a general tendency to inclusiveness on this point. The church is challenged to remember that "if just women, who constitute over 50 percent of the church membership in the United States, could be encouraged and allowed to use their spiritual gifts a tremendous dynamic for growth would be released that now is largely stifled." [70] One would hope that this challenge is more than practical and represents a genuine philosophical commitment. There is not much challenge to leadership roles on the part of women elsewhere in the literature, and so it is difficult to evaluate. I hope it may be understood that women possess the whole range of gifts and are not to be relegated to those "service" roles generally considered to be "women's work" in the church. I fear that the emphasis on women's rights and opportunities will disappear in those situations where it might not be considered successfully utilitarian for them to function. There is some indication that church growth would have us think in terms of the male as the "head of the household" who makes a decision for the entire family and brings them into the church. It is McGavran's belief that Protestantism has placed too much stress on the individual to the neglect of family units. [71] This would be quite in keeping with the tribal mass-movement emphasis found elsewhere in his work. Right now, however, especially in urban areas, there needs to be great concern for the individual. The sociological setting is not at all the same as in the small town assumptions that underlie much of the church growth literature. This tendency to revert to the past as something of an ideal could thwart the very fine recognition of women's gifts which begins to surface in, at least, Wagner's treatment of spiritual gifts. It is a much needed emphasis, and one hopes that more attention may be given in forthcoming materials from the School of World Mission and Institute of Church Growth.

The Body of Christ Primary

The use of gifts is centered in the biblical understanding of the body of Christ, and this understanding undergirds the church growth's concept of the successful church. Biblical religion knows hardly anything at all of a private religion or a confession of faith unrelated to the larger body of believers, i.e., the body that is the church. The Christian call is always a two-fold call: a call unto God and a call unto one another. Paul uses the term "in Christ" or "in the Lord" some two hundred times. At times, this means a mystical union with Christ as a description of intimate and personal fellowship with Christ (Galatians 3:27), as Christ's possession. Most of the time, however, the larger concept is that of being "in the fellowship of Christ," i.e., in the community of Christ.

Thinking in terms of Christ as the representative head, Paul has in mind the corporate personality concept and perceives a shared life, a koinonia bound together with fellow believers. To be a Christian is a social rather than an individual experience. I do not wish to suggest that one does not become a Christian through an individual process. I do want to suggest that the individual is destined to be born into a family.

This fellowship, koinonia, is not so much that of association with other persons, mere togetherness, but a sharing in something which others share, i.e., sharing in the body of Christ. There is no "go it alone" religion. To be "in Christ" is to be part of that body. The key summary is to be found in 1 Corinthians 12, although the same note is likewise in Romans 12. "For just as the body is one and has many members, and all the members of the body, though many, are one body, so it is with Christ" (1 Corinthians 12:12). One can no more live in isolation than a hand can live unconnected with the body.

This does not mean, of course, that there are not times when one should be alone. There is a *soul* time that every individual must have, alone. My hero Christian martyr, Dietrich Bonhoeffer, dealt with the necessity of "the day alone" in his little book *Life Together*. He warned that many even seek fellowship "because they are afraid to be alone." Not being able to stand loneliness, they are driven to the company of other people. He stresses the necessity of solitude and silence and even warns that if one cannot be alone, he or she is not prepared for community. Says he: "Alone you stood before God when he called you; alone you had to answer that call; . . . alone you will die and give an account to God. You cannot escape from yourself; for God has singled you out." [72] But then he makes the reverse statement: "Let him who is not in community beware of being alone."

Bonhoeffer's way of stating the community aspect may sound a bit stringent, but he is right on target when he says:

Into the community you were called, the call was not meant for you alone; in the community of the called you bear your cross, you struggle, you pray. You are not alone, even in death, and on the Last Day you will be only one member of the great congregation of Jesus Christ. If you scorn the fellowship of the brethren, you reject the call of Jesus Christ, and thus your solitude can only be hurtful to you. [73]

And then, he says further, "We recognize, then, that only as we are within the fellowship can we be alone. . . ." [74]

Biblically, theologically, practically, and socially, church growth people have ample background and support for the calling of individuals into the church. The rock on which the church is built is the rock of fellowship in Christ with one another. Part of the trouble in our kind of world is that each insists on standing out there alone, associating only with "his or her kind" while Christ came to draw us all into one family of God.

Parenthetically, it is this very fine emphasis on the body of Christ by church people which makes it difficult for me to understand their harsh emphasis on homogeneity. It is as if they wanted the body composed only of all hands, arms, etc. But that evaluation must come later. It is instructive at this point, however, to look at our Lord's original band of disciples, for it certainly contained a very heterogeneous group with all the elements that make for human friction. There was the cross-cultural relationship of Philip, touched by the Greek culture, and the pure Hebrew, Nathanael. A nationalist like Simon the Zealot found himself yoked with Matthew, a tax collector, whose loyalty was surely in question. Yet they were formed together into a community.

Discipleship is dependent upon the body of Christ concept. The word in the Bible most often used for witness is "servanthood." Leadership in the kingdom of God was given to the one who was prepared to fulfill most perfectly this servant role, a role that deliberately gave up celestial splendor to empty itself and take the form of a servant. Servanthood meant being prepared to wash the disciples' feet, to live without an earthly home, and to be ready to embrace even the cross. We need the church, the body, to demonstrate that pattern. Privatized religion is not prepared to take up that pattern—for that pattern is costly—and privatized religion is primarily interested in receiving, not giving.

The call of Christ is the call of the cross, and, truthfully, we cannot carry the cross alone, but the church, the community of the cross strengthened by the fellowship of the cross, enables the individual to stand. The individual must have the church if there is to be wholeness and growth in life's journey and witness. Since there is the recognition that the individual needs the community, it is most difficult for me to understand how the electronic church people can be such a large part of church growth when the local communities of the electronic church seem to be *only* the springboard for larger ambitions. It is this unholy alliance between church growth and the electronic church that creates a certain mistrust in spite of all the positive qualities, openly stated.

I like the statement of McGavran and Arn when they portray church growth as having "a high view of the church" and view the church not as *a* body of Christ but as *the* body of Christ.[75] There is no churchless ministry apart from a worshiping fellowship, and baptism, a rite of the body, is the symbol of incorporation into that fellowship. The command to baptize is associated with receiving people into the fellowship of the church and anticipates their being in communion.

3

An Evaluation of the Church Growth Movement

Orlando Costas summarizes the sense of expectancy for the church as an anticipation that it shall grow in three ways: in breadth, which has to do with numbers; in depth, which has to do with incorporating people into the fellowship and helping them to mature in the faith; and in height, which has to do with a changed life-style with all of its ethical implications.[1]

This expectant outward thrust and incorporation into the fellowship do appear to be faithful to the pattern of the church's growth as found in the only "history" of the early church that we possess—the book of Acts. The early church was certainly an outward movement that moved to Jewish Christianity (chapters 1–12) and on to Gentile Christianity (chapters 13–28). An almost stereotyped formula occurs throughout Acts (6:7; 9:31; 12:24; 16:5; 19:20; 28:20-31), emphasizing "growth" in the process. Much of the growth emphasis is upon numbers, "the number of disciples in Jerusalem went on increasing rapidly" (6:7, NEB). The book ends, however, with a renewed stress upon the qualitative aspects of growth, for the incorporation into the fellowship was accompanied with "teaching the facts about the Lord Jesus" (28:31, NEB).

The expansion of Christianity as reported in Acts is portrayed in terms of the inward preparation of the church (1:1–2:40) and the outward journey of the church, moving from Jerusalem as the center (2:41–12:25) to Antioch (13:1–19:20) and then to Rome as the center (19:21–28:31). Both the preparation for mission and the process in mission always had a boldness about them. Indeed, this theme of boldness provides a framework for Acts.

The challenged disciples prayed that God would give them boldness (4:29). The book ends with a stress upon the boldness of the mission (28:31). When Peter and John were brought before the chief council of Jerusalem because of their witness, there was amazement at their boldness (4:13*a*). The council credited this boldness to the fact that Peter and John had been companions with Jesus (4:13*b*). The disciples prayed for boldness (4:29) because of the council's prohibition against any further connection with the name (cause) of Christ (4:18).

Certainly the early church grew, but one needs to be cautious about a simple transference from that context, time, and place to the present moment. Above all, one must be cautious about "proof-texting" a definitive methodology for a system based on the picture in Acts. Acts is a story of the spread of centers of Christianity throughout the then known world. It is not a manual on "how to grow churches." There is very little emphasis on methodology. The exciting emphasis has to do with how the church grew and touched the wider world because of the vigorous and fermenting ministry of the Holy Spirit. This movement of the church in the cloister to become the church in the streets is predicated upon the acts of the Holy Spirit. Whether it is in the Jewish phase of Christianity or in the Gentile phase, in all of the stages within each, the Holy Spirit is the motive power and inner life of the witness. When there were difficulties and obstacles, it was not a simple matter of "getting the ten steps for growth" straightened out with a little fixing here and a few adjustments there. If anything is clear, it is that the growth of the early church was not a human enterprise. And herein lies much of my ambivalence toward the technical design of the church growth school. The challenge to have a vision of sharing the gospel is so urgent and there are insights and methods that appear to be so helpful and valuable, but there is such an arrogance about it all. Human activity is at the center of the whole thing, as if technique is the answer. God is at the fringes. We need him, but if the program is right, success is assured. The impression is left ever and again that if the church is not growing, it is simply because we are doing something wrong. But then I notice that if church growth people hit a snag, they are directed simply to remove their effort and their church from these unreceptive people and move someplace else, perhaps to the newer suburban ring. Where is the emphasis upon the obstacles, the antichrists, the call to faithfulness in the midst of difficulties? For those thousands of implanted islands of Christian community already established here and there in difficult places, church growth is more a call to retreat than it is a call to boldness.

Too much of the model is built on the pattern of the expanding corporation rather than on integrated and family-styled communities of faith. The early days of expanding Christianity were primarily centered in a small-group movement where Christians gathered house to house. House churches were the order of the day. This is not to suggest that this should therefore by transference become the pattern of the present. It does bother me, however, that church growth specialists use the book of Acts as their proof for what they are advocating but then portray success in terms of huge churches numbering in the thousands of people for each church. In fairness to church growth people, they do here and there champion the house church "togetherness" as the ideal for the contemporary church and speak of everybody knowing everybody else, caring for one another and loving one another as the household of God.[2] Their literature is devoted, however, to the principle that "bigger is better," and the success examples and allied partners are people like Robert Schuller and Jerry Falwell with churches like Coral Ridge Presbyterian in Florida; First Baptist in Dallas and in Hammond, Indiana; Thomas Road Baptist in Lynchburg; First Nazarene in Denver. These are hardly house churches. The press for bigness tends to nullify the strong biblical emphasis on conversion as entrance (Acts 2:41) and nurture as habitual (2:42-47). If there were the possibility of the church starting its history all over again, it should be warned about the accumulation of huge real estate holdings and buildings of massive size which absorb untold energy and money. Instead of providing a corrective, church growth presents the ideal of bigness in such a way as to perpetuate the mistakes of the institutional church of the past. In a word, many of the ideals presented by church growth are worthy and wholesome, but the push of the methodology is inconsistent with the simplicity of some of the statements.

These are the glaring inconsistencies that create such a sense of discomfort with the movement. There is a kind of biblical literalism about the church growth movement which champions projections and makes claims for itself in such orthodox terms and sounds. But there is a harshness about the methodology which makes one (or causes me, at any rate) to have the feeling that the religious claims in familiar jargon are a surface dressing, often a cover-up, for a rather secular method that works, whether it be in the church or in some other activity.

Biblical Claim for Homogeneity

I do not know of any place that this uneasiness surfaces more intensely than in church growth's so-called biblical claim for homogeneity. Let us face it. It is easier to work with "our kind" where everyone has basically the same roots and cultural tastes, the same prejudices, the same inbred assumption that we are special beyond the next group. But does that easiness make it a mandate? How can the statement "God has made of one blood all . . ." (see Acts 17:26) in any manner be used as a directive for building upon separation? It is gross heresy and sin to suggest that since people have prejudices, those biases should be capitalized upon and made an aid to Christianity.[3]

This argument is part and parcel of the debate that seeks to build a case for apartheid in the Dutch Reformed church of South Africa. The primary argument of this church is that God created diverse peoples with their different cultures and that the church must therefore maintain that diversity. They speak of "unity in diversity" but stress separateness. The Dutch church argues that it has a primary responsibility to evangelize South Africa. Since the blacks and coloreds don't speak Afrikaans, the best way to reach them is through their own churches and own languages. Therefore, separatism has been justified as a means of mission. This again is the argument of church growth. Homogeneity is a practical strategem that works. The danger of this approach is made blatantly clear in the political alliance that the church has made. Nothing could be more evil than the subsequent removal of black people to "homelands" where they must live. Since there is little industry or other means of finding economic support in these homelands, the males must often find menial work many miles away where they live in substandard conditions, earn money to send back home, and maybe get home one month out of the year. The deterioration of family life and the horrible moral and social problems that have resulted from such a practice are a matter of public record. The next step has been to declare that any relationship between blacks and whites is a sin since God made them that way and they ought to associate with "their own kind of people." Politically and socially this has resulted in all kinds of humiliation as blacks have been excluded from large facets of life with "white only" toilets, restaurants, beaches, hotels, churches, etc. Once the practice was established, the church then picked through the Bible trying to find some justification. This is exactly what the church growth people have done. The evil of the homogeneous system is then compounded by an eisegesis that purports to give biblical authority to the system.

This gross pragmatism is very obvious in a small publication authored by J. Robertson McQuilkin of Moody Institute, *How Biblical Is the Church Growth Movement?* He suggests that the movement was born of "scientific observation" and involves pragmatic considerations. Then he asks a question which he proceeds to answer: "Why is it necessary for a demonstrably successful method to be analyzed and interrogated in the light of Scripture?"[4] He makes a "biblical search" seeking to justify church growth practices. Support is thus found for homogeneity; God's selective concern for some and not for others and various other practices are found. This is the pattern of the South African church in abusing the Bible. It is also the pattern that was used in the South in the United States for over one hundred years. Many years ago I had spoken at a gathering in Alabama and then was taken as a courtesy to meet the governor and other dignitaries in Montgomery. As I was leaving, a judge gave me a pamphlet entitled "The Other Side of the Civil War." A native southerner myself, I read it with interest. Prejudice against black people was justified on the basis of the "curse" upon Canaan in Genesis 9:25. Here, the pamphlet argued, was just punishment for Canaan's sin and the beginning of a subservient black race. To say nothing of the fact that the writers confused the family lines as given in Genesis, the argument is an example of how the Bible is so easily abused in finding support for "something that works." So it is that the principle of homogeneity, so stringently pursued, causes biblical abuse, confirms prejudices against others, and undergirds the tendency to arrogance over those "not like us."

Church growth people often refer to the work of Southern Baptists and point to their numerical success as a verification and justification of the homogeneous principle. As a former Southern Baptist, I believe this cultural maintenance and cultural isolation to be one of their greatest weaknesses. These churches have been so successful because they are a reflection, almost an exact replica, of the societal culture about them. The church makes "religious" what already exists in the world. In spite of this "cheap grace" and blessing of culture, there are many strengths that Southern Baptists have to share. Their zeal and programmatic genius are something to behold. Their acclaimed (although distorted) love for the Bible is second to none. They have many strengths to share but cannot share them because they are geared primarily to work with their "own kind." This is not to overlook their increasing work with minorities in urban centers, but even this work is done by transporting a certain cultural pattern to the new areas, a cultural pattern that is not likely to hold across the generations.

This homogeneous principle gives sanctity to the unholy *status quo* and applauds it as routine. Church growth advocates encourage the church to identify the given culture as "my" culture. This is surely a "sell out" for a gospel that often calls one "to leave father and mother, brother and sister." This baptism of culture on the basis of the success pattern of homogeneity is "a new version of the old Constantinism."[5] Immediate success may well be a prelude to a horrible disaster in bringing into the church large numbers of baptized unbelievers whose societal biases have been confirmed and made respectable by a "system that works."

Of course one should be aware of social and cultural structures. Attention must be given to cultural factors that stimulate or impede the sharing of the gospel, but these must not be blessed and concretized and made the basis of a theory. The success of the theory will ever mitigate changing cultural evil. Such separatism creates and perpetuates all kind of disharmony, and the Bible is called upon for its defense.

It seems preposterous to me that church growth people should go to the table of nations in Genesis 10 and the Tower of Babel in Genesis 11 as indications that "social pluralism was part of God's creational plan," and the belief that "there is no hint that God had intended anything else for the people he had created to populate the earth"[6] is outrageous. Genesis is no more a sociological treatise on what ought to be than it is a scientific treatise on how the world came into being. Sociological descriptions in the Bible represent a perception from a particular writer's vantage point, and the sociological description is only part of a vehicle that seeks to portray a religious or theological understanding of God's relationship with humankind. Genesis 1–11 is a theological preface to the remainder of Genesis, indeed, to the remainder of the Old Testament. Disharmony and fragmentation in one's relationship with God (Genesis 1–3) creates disharmony and fragmentation in one's relationship with his or her brother or sister (the Cain and Abel narratives in Genesis 4). Chapter 11 is a summary chapter that draws together the threads of the previous ten chapters in an illustrative way. There is certainly no effort here to champion separation on the basis of a homogeneous unit principle.

The point being made is that fragmentation in a relationship with God brings fragmentation within community. The basic sin portrayed is that of *hubris*, the self-centeredness that draws all things unto oneself. The fragmentation and splintering into separate groups is the exact opposite of what God desired. Chapter 11, rather than championing separateness as church growth people claim, presents separateness as the result of human sin.

To refer to the composition of the inner circle of Jesus, mostly Galileans, as evidence that the church must be built on the homogeneous principle is about as farfetched as saying that women cannot be priests because Jesus was a male figure. To support the ''rightness'' of homogeneity in pointing to Judas as the lone Judean is too much. Does this mean that if Jesus had been smart enough to have a completely homogeneous unit, there would have been neither betrayal nor crucifixion? To cite the choice of Matthias, a Galilean (Acts 1:23-26), as a corrective to this previous failure in homogeneity is surely farfetched.[7]

Nor can I understand the attempt to justify homogeneity by appealing to the preaching of Jesus and his disciples as being ''confined largely to their own homogeneous unit among the provincial or non-republican, peoples of that narrow 'backwater,' Galilee.''[8] We have to begin where we are. Are we to neglect the journey to Jerusalem and the very significant ministry in between? Perhaps the disciples would have argued for the homogeneous principle. The people whom they encountered on the journey to Jerusalem were not Galileans but Samaritans, Judeans, and others. They were often quite a contrast to the disciples themselves. However, the homogeneous principle was precisely what Jesus condemned. The episode with the Samaritan woman at the well (John 4) is a direct contradiction of the disciples' desire to maintain homogeneous purity. The very crucifixion of Jesus is directly due to his effront to the establishment by deliberately crossing cultural, racial, political, economic, social, and all other kinds of barriers.

The hinge of material used to support homogeneity in church growth is taken from the Jerusalem Conference turmoil in Acts 15. The compromises reached there can hardly be looked upon as a confirmation of God's "separating" will, as many of the church growth adherents would have us do. It is another of those instances of describing "what is" as a mandate for what must be. The book of Acts and especially Acts 15 do indeed indicate that every group must be able to respond to the gospel in terms of its own culture. At the same time, it does not establish a cleavage between groups but removes all cleavage. The book of Acts demonstrates that Christianity is a universal religion for all people of every country, bridging every difference that human beings can know. Philip preaching to Samaritans, Stephen making Christianity a universal thing and being killed for it, Peter accepting Cornelius into the church, Jewish Christians preaching to Gentiles at Antioch—all of these are cementing a universal family relationship rather than building islands of people separated from others. The recognition of the different culture practices is not a mandate of method but a stress upon acceptance.

If anything, Acts 15 is a challenge to the Jews to relinquish their cultural exclusiveness and cultural isolationism. The Jerusalem Conference was to break down barriers and not to confirm them. We are dealing with attitudes. The Jews thought themselves to be the peculiar possession of God, and God was felt to be the peculiar possession of the Jews. Jews had lived with the idea that a Jew could not receive a Gentile as a guest in the house, and certainly a Jew would not do business with a Gentile. The question is whether we hold back our approval until people become what we want. The answer is that unqualified love receives people into one another's fellowship regardless of their cultural definitions. The purpose of Acts 15 certainly is *not* to confirm the necessity of separate fellowship. In Acts 15 the expansion of the gospel is at stake, but the quality of fellowship is also at stake. Grace overcomes barriers. Acts 15 does not demand worship in a particular style, but neither does it forbid worship in a particular style. The problem was whether Gentiles had to subscribe to the same requirements as Jews. The answer was that there are no legalistic and stylistic requirements. The answer was not, "You must remain separate in order to grow." That, of course, was not the question. Thus, using Acts 15 to confirm homogeneity is seeking to apply the experience to a question that was not being asked. Gentiles and Jews were to be on the same footing with no difference at all. The fellowship was to include all cultures, not separate them into different cultures. Acts 15 might be used as an argument *against* homogeneity and not as a substantiation for it.

Regardless of where one puts the book of Galatians in relation to Acts 15, the emphasis is similar. Paul's reprimand of Peter who participated in or refused table fellowship according to who might be watching (Galatians 2:11-14) is not directed toward separateness. Peter himself in the defense of his mission to Cornelius (Acts 10–11) had already established the principle that barriers fall where the Lord is. Peter thought he had been obedient to Christ before, but "in his vision on the housetop his self-image as an obedient Christian was shattered."[9] He discovered that he was not truly obedient *until* he *crossed* cultural lines and went to Cornelius. It would appear that the entire emphasis of Scripture is that life in Christ transcends barriers. Therefore, to take these different settings that undergird the acceptance of all and to use those settings to build a system of methodology which is homogeneous appears to violate the very spirit of the Scripture itself.

Such a strict insistence upon homogeneity would have denied Paul's mission as an apostle to the Gentiles. Once again he set out to cross barriers and build bridges, for Christ was about the same thing. Had his purpose been to confirm barriers, his apostleship should have been entrusted into the hands of a Gentile. Even in those biblical settings where you have primarily a Jewish community or a Gentile community, it is one thing to say that all such communities of faith are to be accepted and quite something else to say that such homogeneous communities must be the pattern for all other fellowships of faith.

To insist on homogeneous units is to miss the growing awareness that this is God's cosmos in which there are no natural barriers. When one of our first astronauts was circling the universe, he said that the thing that impressed him so much and gave him such a tremendous sense of reverence was the realization that, as he looked down upon the globe, there were no national boundaries. It was just one world, without division, God's cosmos, and he realized that all of the divisions had been made by human beings. Crossing cultural barriers is right at the heart of the Christian gospel, and the rejection of the barriers that divide people is basic to the new community in Christ (Ephesians 2:11-21). I cannot imagine that, at a time when secularization is contributing to the sense of humanness that recognizes that humankind should not be divided into artificial divisons, the church should be going in the direction of "blessing" such divisions.

This stress on homogeneity creates an attitude of separateness that goes hand in hand with a lack of concern, if not a prejudice against, those outside our own milieu. It is reprehensible to me that Wagner should use the doctrine of creation in an attempt to maintain the homogeneous principle. He asks a series of questions: "Why is there so much diversity in the world to begin with? Is there some theological rationale for it? Is the extensive pluralism characteristic of the human race today part of the creative purposes of God?"[10] To ask such questions with the implied "God did it" reminds me of the intense resistance to the issues of the civil rights struggle in the fifties and sixties by my relatives and friends in the South who insisted that if God had intended for black and white to be together, God would have made us all one color or another. Of course a multiplicity of cultures has a variety of strengths to contribute to the whole. Of course, the distinctiveness of those cultural contributions should be recognized. That contribution, however, is all the more reason for heterogeneity of association rather than a homogeneous isolation where the potential sharing of those strengths is denied. The maintenance of barriers between cultures contributes to the sense of exclusivity so that each unit begins to feel that it does not need what the other has to contribute because it is probably inferior anyway. The demonic championing of a superior master race under Hitler is a perverse extension of this principle, and the two hundred years of black slavery on the American scene is another possible aberration. Homogeneity misses the major note of reconciliation as a key theme of the Christian gospel, breaking down walls of petition between male and female, Jew and Greek, or whomever or whatever. The body of Christ should not be merely a reflection of the divisions that exist on earth, "predetermined by the exterior similarity of social class and cultural background."[11] I think I must agree that where the church has insisted on remaining homogeneous, even though it may have grown in the process, that failure to embrace all of Christ's family is a judgment rather than a commendation. The call of Christ is more of a call to separate from the world as *it is* and model what the new creation ought to be. It is of little value to describe the old world and the old order with all of its diversity when the eschatological expectation brings the pressure of the future upon the present in order to transform the present into God's tomorrow. That means that the church will likely be quite unlike its culture. Of course this transformation is much more difficult than "baptizing the culture," and the very difficulty may make it less numerically successful. While we do not place a premium on smaller numbers, there may be times when this is what will result from faithfulness to the vision of a new creation.

But now I must summarize this long excursion and give it focus. It is interesting that so much stress is placed on homogeneity in the church growth movement. Yet for his examples of the strategy for growth, McGavran goes to the synagogue where Jews and Gentiles are gathered together.[12] Does this mean that non-Christian groups can associate on a heterogeneous basis but Christian groups cannot? He stresses "looking for people already included," but obviously these Gentile proselytes to Judaism were included in a Jewish setting. In the name of success, is the Christian ethic to be less mature than the Jewish one that preceded it? Likewise, if homogeneity is an absolute must, it seems strange to me that a Philip could have felt any mandate to deal with the Samaritans who were socially at a great distance or a Paul with Gentiles.

McGavran and Arn indicate that the Great Commission brought about the church's social expansion after its initial geographical expansion. According to their reckoning, the churches in Jerusalem and Judea were composed primarily of commoners, "ignorant and unlearned men." But these commoners continued to pray for and work with the upper class until a great number of priests were added to the church. The understanding of the Great Commission was developed further, and then a large number of proselytes became Christians.[13] Their point, of course, is that social gaps were continually crossed until there was a wide horizon of believers covering every class of people in the early church. This tracing of the Christian movement to new social groups seems to be diametrically opposed to the principle of homogeneity and counterproductive to church growth arguments that the only way to grow a church is with "our kind of people."

Of all the writers in the church growth stable, Charles Mylander does give evidence of some doubts about homogeneity and begins to open the door to reconsideration. He asks the question, "Are homogeneous churches really Christian?" He answers that they are only if they remain open to other groups who want to hear the gospel and join the church. Open hearts and open doors must embody the spirit of Galatians 3:28, oneness in Christ. He then admits that in the development of biblical religion "Gentiles from other homogeneous groups did join the covenant people of God from time to time, but to do so, they had to leave their own cultural people and cross the social barriers to join Israel."[14] Although these Gentiles did join themselves to a basically homogeneous unit, Israel, it does show that crossing social and cultural gaps was not and is not out of the question. Can we expect any less of Christian groups? Although there were problems, to be sure, we know that the early Christian community in Jerusalem was heterogeneous with Judeans, Galileans, and Hellenists (Acts 6). Ultimately some Gentiles were also included. Although the result of the Jerusalem Conference in Acts 15 may have been the freedom of homogeneous units (Jew and Gentile) to develop their own styles, this admission was but a prelude to the mixing of styles. Mylander exhibits another qualm of conscience about the homogeneous principle when he suggests that where there are homogeneous units, these need to cooperate with different homogeneous units and share different styles and preferences on the intercongregational level, and he advocates fellowship with Christians of different homogeneous units.[15] If cooperation is possible on one level, it is possible on all levels. One does not have to lose one's cultural identity or ethnicity in order to live and worship together, as church growth people assume. It will be shared as a strength, and the whole becomes richer in the process. The crack in homogeneity appears again when Mylander agrees that "sociological factors do not cause growth, but they can thwart it."[16] Of course that is true. Christian communities are not trouble-free, and differences do have to be handled. This, however, is part of the journey toward oneness in Christ. Totally homogeneous units in terms of race, social class, education, etc., are not trouble-free either. Some of the worst wrangles in the world are among "our kind of people" whose ego goals confict one with another. Church growth people seem increasingly to recognize that multi-congregational approaches may be a possibility, patterned somewhat on the work of North Shore Baptist Church in Chicago or Temple Baptist Church in Los Angeles. They also indicate that ethnic congregations should be part of "regular" denominations that have a great mix of constituents. Thus, when pressed to the total picture of the Christian community, there are inconsistencies in the homogeneous argument. I think the inconsistencies appear because the advocates are trying to take what they believe to be a sociological principle, in their view—scientifically tested—and superimpose it upon the biblical material. They get into trouble when they find support in some places but great challenge in the larger context. There is much to be gleaned concerning the difficulties involved in building Christian community, but these difficulties should not therefore become the reason for a compromised mandate, which would reduce Christian community to the lowest possible denominator.

Failure of Social Concern

An inevitable result of building around units of separateness is the lack of concern for those who are not like us and the blunting of the social thrust of the gospel. That is, of course, just what church growth people advocate. They do not want social action at all and state quite categorically: "To the degree that socially involved churches become engaged in social action, as distinguished from social service, they can expect church growth to diminish." [17] The primary thrust must be upon the "multiplication of cells of Christians," and the church growth venture considers the social order as contrary to the task. Supporting social causes, so they say, gives mixed signals, and no mixed signals are desired. Social service is given a sub-subpriority, but, says Wagner, "I hesitate to classify social action as any priority for churches—as churches—at all." [18] That, of course, is but another way of speaking the old adage, "Play it safe."

A sharp distinction is made between "service" and "mission." It is admitted that we have some responsibility to help the sick, teach the ignorant, and do what we can to bring about human betterment, but that is just something all should do and is not part of the church's mission. According to the church growth philosophy, service projects cannot be part of mission. [19] The proof text for this differentiation is the election of deacons in Acts 6, people who, according to Tippett, were engaged in service projects and not in mission. However, a careful following of the deacons in their preaching and evangelizing will lead to the discovery that the deacons did not know of any such differentiation. Nonetheless, it is suggested that "pastors of growing churches avoid even mentioning the burning social issues of the day in their pulpits." [20] Robert Schuller, church growth's bright star, openly advocates the elimination of anything from one's preaching program which can cause the least bit of controversy or discomfort. His basic thesis is that in order to be successful in growing a church, a pastor must never, never say anything unpleasant, must eschew the prophetic stance, and always send people away feeling good.[21] On this count, every major prophet would have scored a miserable failure, and those like Jeremiah and especially Micah and Amos would never have been included in the canon.

One of the major reasons for denying the legitimacy of the social concerns of the gospel is that such an involvement disturbs homogeneity and creates great discomfort, especially for the middle class, and church growth techniques are especially geared to middle-class comfort. Great store is placed in church growth materials on finding biblical support for one principle or another. It is therefore necessary to examine this failure of social concern from a biblical context. This needs to be done by understanding something of the troubled times in which people live and then inquiring whether there are biblical directives that both focus and require the church's concern.

In our own country the very system that has blessed many has also been a curse upon others. From our beginning days we have assumed a policy of economic expansion, assuming that nature is generous beyond limit. We have assumed that if a person just worked hard enough, he or she would move up in the world. We have assumed that the entire social good would be helped if each individual pursued his or her own personal self-interest. We have assumed that material progress best defines who a person is, and we have chased that progress without giving thought to the depletion of the world's resources and without thought of what we might be depriving future generations. Growth became our secular religion and happiness, primarily defined in material terms, has centered on the circle of the self. Now that same kind of growth and theme of comfort, happily associating with our kind, has carried over into the church.

The result of such a pattern, exclusive of concern for those outside our circle, is that at least 25 million of our people are at the poverty level and unrest grows again in our cities, the unrest which for the most part church growth is willing to neglect, and the unrest of which revolutions are made.

This philosophy of growth expansion has at least been a contributing factor to the troubled world at large where two-thirds of the world is in poverty and frustration and where the gap between the various "kinds" grows wider rather than smaller. Can it possibly be right for the church to settle into its "own kind" and not care about the "other kind"? Do church people have no ethical and moral responsibility when multinational corporations make huge investments and justify them by what is poured into national economies, mostly to those who already "have," in which the little people profit hardly at all while they watch the irreplaceable natural resources taken away? The roots of wealth of rich countries are buried deep in the third world.[22] The troubled people, not "our kind," are increasingly restless. Iran may be only one small example of many explosions as people seek to free themselves. Even where there is political freedom, there is no true liberation unless there is also economic freedom. Is it then the church's purpose to go and "save" these people for heaven with no responsibility for saving them from the perils of wretchedness and misery in this world?

What is our concern? As we recognize that biblical religion in both Testaments is concerned about the little people of the earth, does this not bring us to the task of the church? We need to recognize that the Old Testament has much to say about the powerless. The prophets often spoke to the powerful, like kings (Jeremiah 22) and other prophets (Jeremiah 23 and Micah 3:5) and establishment priests (Micah 3:11) and judges. And they spoke to them about the powerless and dispossessed and cut-off people (Isaiah 3:13-15; 10:1-2; Amos 2:6f.; 4:4). This concern was rooted in Old Testament law, which provided that the tithe collected be used to take care of the needs of the poor, not to keep up church property (Deuteronomy 14:28-29; 26:12-15). Even when it meant crossing barriers, they were to be kind and generous to these poor ones (Deuteronomy 15:7-11) and bring them into the faith community (Deuteronomy 16:9-15). The historical books express similar concern. A primary stress in the little book of Ruth is that gleanings are left for the poor. The wisdom literature is pointed in its concern. Such emphatic statements meet us as "he who closes his ear to the cry of the poor will himself cry out and not be heard" (see Proverbs 21:13; 22:9; 29:7; 14:21; 14:31; 19:17; 31:20; 29:14; 31:9). We are even told that the Lord will plead their cause.[23]

That this concern for the dispossessed—the widow, the orphan, and the poor—is central to what is expected in the life-style of a people who calls itself the people of God is continued in the New Testament. Jesus in Matthew 25 makes such concern and action the test of whether one is a Christian, a member of the kingdom. The primary definition of religion that the New Testament offers is to be found in the book of James: "Religion that is pure and undefiled before God and the Father is this: to visit orphans and widows in their affliction, and to keep oneself unstained from the world" (James 1:27). Religion for the people of God thus becomes a very practical matter when to say "Go in peace" is not enough when one needs food and clothing (James 2:14-16).

It is demonic for a church to major on growth when primary focus in certain settings should be on another kind of mission. It is in Luke's Gospel that I find my strongest corrective when I am tempted to think that social concern for the church is irrational and political, especially in that section (Luke 1:46-55) that we have come to call the "Magnificat" from Mary:

He has shown strength with his arm,
he has scattered the proud in the imagination of their hearts,
he has put down the mighty from their thrones,
and exalted those of low degree;
he has filled the hungry with good things,
and the rich he has sent empty away.

—Luke 1:51-53

This is that which Jesus confirmed both at the beginning and the end of his ministry. At the inaugural sermon in Nazareth (Luke 4), Jesus said, in effect, "God has anointed me to preach good news to the poor; he has sent me to proclaim release to the captives, and recovery of sight to the blind, to set at liberty those who are oppressed" (v. 18). The emphasis at the conclusion of his ministry is very clear in Matthew 25.

But it is in Luke's Gospel more than anyplace else that God's care for the crippled and rejected members of society is emphasized. As Killinger suggests:

> From the song of the angels to the poor, semireligious shepherds on the hillsides (Luke 2:8-20) to Jesus' promise of Paradise to the criminal next to him at the crucifixion (Luke 23:42-43); from the Master's announcement in Nazareth that his ministry was for the poor, sick, and oppressed (Luke 4:14-30) to his controversial decision to dine with Zacchaeus, the outcaste tax collector (Luke 19:1-10), the unfailing orientation of the Gospel is toward the weak, the lost, and the despised.[24]

Dietrich Bonhoeffer reminded us that the church is asked to look at the world from the perspective of those who are the outcasts, the mistreated, and the sufferers, for therein we discover that the protests of the poor may be the voice of God.

Mary herself spoke out as one of the common folk of Palestine in the context of a church that was concerned primarily with itself and with its own well-being, just as church growth people are advocating such self-concern in the rejection of any outward thrust that does not contribute to numerical increase. Hers was a land of shocking poverty, overcrowded, ravaged with hunger, and terribly demanding upon its poor resources of food and water. Yet God walked with these simple folk of the countryside where currents of faithful religion ran deep.

Jesus himself as a homeless refugee being carried into Egypt provides the image that "it is [often] precisely among the homeless and unwanted of the world that the love of God dwells in its incarnate form."[25] Surely God does call the church as the continuing incarnation to extend the ministry that was so important to Jesus himself. Rather than to suggest that this is not the church's responsibility, the New Testament (Matthew 25) suggests that it is the very criterion by which membership in the kingdom is determined. To deny the social thrust of the gospel in the name of the numerical success of the church is to make membership in a church more important than membership in the kingdom.

One of the claims that is made by church growth advocates is that the church cannot be involved in both social concern and evangelism, that the two are mutually exclusive. Walter Rauschenbusch, the so-called "father of the social gospel," placed a great stress upon individual salvation and was insistent that the call to a reception of Christ be clearly issued:

> If the new interest in social questions crowds out the old interest in evangelistic work, it is a reaction from an old one-sidedness into a new one-sidedness. Social redemption must prove its truth and higher spiritual efficiency by presenting stronger motives and working out wiser methods of evangelism than any heretofore. . . . Nothing can supersede that great experience when the soul of man consciously turns to God.[26]

He called people to decision concerning the crucified and risen Lord. If anything, Rauschenbusch was more evangelistic than some of the church growth people who minimize any calling to decision lest it imply that they individually must come away from something and cross uncomfortable barriers to Christ.

The sixties in this country are sometimes cited as the rationale for presenting social concern as counterproductive to growth. It must be admitted that the church often failed during those turbulent times. In many instances she became so concerned about the small Band-aids being placed on huge gaping wounds that she neglected internal nurture. The call to provide a presence in the midst of chaos did often short-circuit the call to the church. Unfortunately there had been a vacuum in the church's ministry to the world. It has often occurred in the history of the church that in seeking to offer a corrective to our blindness in certain areas, we neglect areas that were important before. This has created a new heresy. This failure does not therefore mean that the church is called to one or the other. It does mean that the church is called to balance. No matter how much an institution may grow numerically, if it neglects to contribute to the liberation of humankind in all walks of life, that successful institution is something less than the church. The inward journey and the outward journey are both the mission of the church. Faithfulness to the gospel has such accompanying signs as demonstrating genuine concern for the world about us. Orlando Costas puts it all together when he suggests that "the true test of mission is not whether we proclaim, make disciples or engage in social, economic and political liberation, but whether we are capable of integrating all three in a comprehensive, dynamic *and consistent* witness."[27] Of course some people resist this integration of mission and hold back because of it. May God help us, however, if we reduce the claims of the gospel in order to bring people, at no cost, into something that confirms the selfish life-style and makes it "OK" because it is now surrounded by religious paraphernalia.

We are too easily capable of such cheap grace. Recently I was surveying some of the programs offered under the aegis of the so-called "electronic church." The male impresario of one of the programs was away, and his spouse was "M.C." for the hour. Her dress and movements and mannerisms were hardly different from what would have been found at the local discotheque. The music of which she was a part was just as sensual and suggestive. The promise that came through again and again was that if the viewer would just "take Jesus," that viewer could have the "good life," and the good life was presented in terms of having the things of this world. It was the American success orientation dressed in a Sunday suit. The reduction of the claims of the cross to cheap shibboleths is a betrayal of the gospel in the name of growth and success. To build around units of separateness that feed the "me" to the exclusion of concern for others is something less than the call of Christ.

The Distortion of Discipleship

Church growth often responds to some of the challenges just discussed by pointing out their differentiation between discipleship and perfecting. Elsewhere in this work I have been most appreciative of church growth's contribution to small-group work, the growth of laity, and other emphases that have to do with Christian nurture. There is something demonic, however, in the church growth challenge first to get people in the church and then to work on changing them after capturing them. People are likely to keep the prejudices with which they were admitted. A certain legitimacy to attitudes is given when they are accepted without challenge. I can hardly think of anything less promising than hordes of people whose attitudes have been "baptized" into acceptance. Of course, spiritual growth is a lifelong process, and reaching maturity is a journey that we never complete. However, if people have not at least heard the claims of discipleship (i.e., "perfecting") before they sign on the dotted line, the likelihood of change is minimal. To present such claims at a later time is likely to result in the feeling that one has been "psychologically manipulated at the point of entry." [28] The parabolic and other literature of the New Testament finds Jesus insisting that one must know the cost of entering the kingdom before one seeks to enter. Evangelism involves confession, and conversion involves a change of direction and the surrender to a new will, which has all kinds of moral and ethical implications. These issues must be raised before one says yes. Herein we have problems with the "people movement" method of bringing people into the church. It is certainly appropriate to understand the group mind and social solidarity and to be as wise as possible in social perceptivity when presenting the claims of the gospel. This method reminds me very much of the situation, however, when my two daughters, as children, were in a certain vacation church school. The assistant pastor marched the entire unit, some several hundred strong, into the auditorium on "Decision Day." The conditions were just right, the peer pressure was operating, and almost the entire number made "decisions for Christ." There was great rejoicing about how the "Spirit had worked." It was indeed a "people movement." My wife and I were furious because minimal inquiry indicated that our daughters, along with most of the others, had failed to comprehend what was taking place except that "everybody did it." Although larger numbers will be gathered through this method, the ultimate damage to the church and the cause of Christ is frightening. Reparation of this damage would require a Reformation all over again. The call of Christ may be so often a call against the group and a call to a way of life totally foreign to anything known before. This is not something that you "slip up" on people in a later process of perfecting after you have brought them in. One cannot expect to take place in a moment what the New Testament presents as a lifelong process. However, to fail to point out the requirement of commitment to a lifelong process and what that lifelong commitment involves is both disillusioning and dishonest, no matter how "success-oriented" it may be.

Furthermore, it must be made very clear that there is something wrong with any call to the love of Christ that does not at the same time involve a call to the love of others, with all that that implies in terms of ethics and spirit. Loving one's enemies, for instance, is part of being a child of God (Matthew 5:43-48). One does not enter the church and then discover somewhere along the line that one can be a child of the kingdom.

The Church Versus the Kingdom

But this, too, presents part of the problem with church growth: the entire case for the church growth movement appears to be built upon a call to the church rather than upon a call to the kingdom of God. I do not like to have to make the differentiation, and surely the church is part of the kingdom, but it is also something less than the kingdom. The newness in the gospel is that the kingdom of God is at hand. The call is to the kingdom of which the church is a part and not a call to the church of which the kingdom is a part. The kingdom call is a call to a radically new allegiance to a radically new Lord. This is not at all to minimize the body of Christ, the people of God, the church with which this book began in chapter 1. It is to remind us, however, that as the body of Christ, we are kingdom individuals with a new citizenship and new demands. The emphasis is not on how easy but on how costly it is to enter the kingdom.

The reign (kingdom) of God must be central for the church even as it was central in the life and teaching of Jesus. His ministry begins with the announcement that "the time is fulfilled, and the kingdom of God is at hand; repent, and believe in the gospel" (Mark 1:15). It concludes with a pointing to the kingdom at the Lord's Supper (Mark 14:25), and the theme of the kingdom of God is the constant theme between the beginning and the end, as the parables will demonstrate. The theme of that kingdom is ever about reconciliation and new life with God. The primary call is to the kingdom of God. The evangelistic message is the proclamation of the Good

News of Jesus Christ and an invitation to respond to him. Churches are a result of the response to the kingdom. Of course, the two, kingdom and church, are closely related. Planting churches is second, however, and not first. It is imperative, therefore, that we keep the primary goal in view. To do so will cause an emphasis somewhat different than that of the church growth school. The passion for numbers and church planting is so all-consuming that the demands of the kingdom are receiving secondary attention. Over a long period of time, this will produce something that is not only less than the kingdom, but also less than the church.

The church growth emphasis upon "discipling," merely getting people into the church with a goal of "perfecting" them later needs to be evaluated in light of such reminders as that from Matthew, "Not every one who says to me, 'Lord, Lord,' shall enter the kingdom of heaven, but he who does the will of my Father who is in heaven" (7:21).

Although the final triumph of God comes through the gradual transformation of humanity, the real message is that divine intervention is not a future hope but a present reality, as experienced through the intervention of Jesus. Whenever and wherever an individual responds to Jesus Christ, the kingdom is present. It is important that the kingdom be present both "within the midst of" and within the life of an individual before that individual is planted in a church that is fruit and evidence of the kingdom. The parables of growth in the New Testament are parables of growth of the kingdom, kingdom parables and not church parables.

The portrait of the kingdom individual (the Sermon on the Mount in Matthew) is of the person who has experienced a realization of need (the poor in spirit, 5:3). Such realization is followed by or accompanied by repentance (they that mourn, 5:4). Realization and repentance are followed by trust (5:5), otherwise the deep sense of need and contrition leave one with a vacuum, in worse condition than before. Trust is derived from the concept of meekness, a word that indicates a willingness to be disciplined and harnessed, guided by another. Salvation (5:6) is the net result. Such an entrance into the kingdom places a content and substance in the new life. Sharing mercy (5:7) becomes the social ethic by which we relate to others. This social ethic is motivated by an inner truth (purity of heart, 5:8). The kingdom individual in turn communicates a compelling evangelism as one engages in peacemaking, i.e., sharing the life of wholeness with others (5:9). This means that vicarious suffering (5:10) is part of the content of that life if such is needed in service to others. This summary of the content of the kingdom individual's life is quite other than the easy church growth picture that requires no crossing of cultural or other barriers but presents a road made easy in order to get people into the church. That message of sacrifice is even more intensified when the call to walk before the world is recognized as demanding a life that is a conserving and flavoring force (salt, 5:13) and that serves as a guiding force (light, 5:16) for all others. The remainder of Matthew 5, verses 17-48, is concerned with the social ethics of the kingdom in respecting the rights of others.

The point of the preceding is that the kingdom determines the nature of the church. Most of Christ's teaching deals with the nature of one's response to the kingly rule of God and the nature of the new life that accompanies that response. Church growth material skips most of the kingdom emphasis. The end result, if left uncorrected, will be nothing less than disastrous. A radical revolution is called for, and this is far different from the pablum that seeks to make people comfortable so that one can get them into the net. One enters the church only because he or she has agreed to live under the kingly rule of God.

Gaining that kingdom is the most important thing in life. It is worth every sacrifice, whether it be of body (eye, Matthew 5:29; hand, Matthew 5:30) or of possessions (Matthew 16:26; Luke 9:25). Jesus understood the human predicament as living outside of the rule of God, being associated with pride, greed, and selfishness. The primary need is to overcome the estrangement from God and others caused by "sin" (a word Schuller does not like), and all of this demands an experience of reconciliation. This reconciliation is a reconciliation with God, self, and the world, a theme that I have treated elsewhere.[29] Such reconciliation demands the crossing of many bridges and overcoming barriers. It can never, even at initial entrance, be satisfied with the "blessing" of those barriers. The Good News is not only that we have someone to love us but also that we have someone to love. All the way through the Gospels, and especially in Mark's Gospel, is a cross experience that encounters sin at its worst and love at its best.

The result of this reconciliation is a new life of holy obedience to the will of God. All of life is turned around, shaken up, made different. Maintaining barriers and easy transition within "people movements" and a satisfaction with old separatisms all seem so foreign to the kingdom life that Jesus presents. Never is Jesus satisfied with salvation to a "next" life someplace. A reconciled person simply is not the same person he or she has been. The transformation within is accompanied by a transformation without (". . . you will know them by their fruits," Matthew 7:15-20). This new wine cannot be stored in old wineskins; a new patch cannot be placed on old garments (Luke 5:36-37). Simply said, although difficult to determine, this transformed life is a life lived under the will of God. This will changes all of life and draws us into a redeeming engagement with the inhumanity and lostness of our world. This engagement involves social and ethical imperatives that compel the church to become involved in the "redemptive participation in the mission of Jesus."

The strain between church and kingdom is derived from church growth's distinction between "discipling" and "perfecting," already mentioned as two different stages in the spiritual experience. McGavran would seek gradually to move the individual from the church stage to the kingdom stage. Here again we have a reversal of the New Testament pattern. Furthermore, it is anticipated that some of those who have been swept in will not respond to this "perfecting" process and will fall away. Will this rejection of the process "constitute a kind of psychological 'vaccination' so that such persons would be less likely to be won in the future than if they had not been discipled in the first place?" is the question raised by John H. Yoder of Associated Mennonite Biblical Seminaries. He further suggests that the children of those who did not make it from church to kingdom, from discipling to perfecting will also more than likely be immune to the process so that the ultimate net result of church growth is again negative.[30]

This confusion relating to church discipling and kingdom perfecting is directly related to the success orientation, which is directly related to the management orientation of the American-style Madison Avenue techniques. We cannot assume as some church growth people do that "you can make Christians the way you make cars and sausages."[31] Regulated machinery and mass production are not the way to do it. I fear that the ultimate damage will be so severe as to impair seriously the mission of the church in the years to come. There is no question that McGavran's motivation is good. Nevertheless, method must not be allowed to supersede biblical and theological faithfulness. To reverse the New Testament pattern in this way is more than a well-intentioned mistake. It is the germinal seed of heresy.

Church first, kingdom second is more of the "it works" syndrome, but a short-term success is hardly worth forfeiting the kingdom. To relinquish the disciplined demands of the kingdom is to foster the "anything goes" attitude that is already evident in the literature. This evidence of flippancy about serious things is illustrated, for instance, by Wagner's light comments on baptism:

Some dip them three times forward and some dip them three times backward. Quakers don't believe in water baptism at all. My own church, a Congregational Church, doesn't think any of this is essential so we baptize both infants and adults by either sprinkling or immersion, and I suppose if someone requested it we would baptize them three times forward. If some don't want to be baptized at all, we also accept them and love them on the same basis as others.[32]

The kingdom is not to be changed at will, nor is the basic nature of the church to be altered by whether something works by simply turning the "right screw." Neither the church nor the kingdom is so mechanical as when Mylander had problems and testified, "I returned and made a couple of changes, and our church began to grow."[33] There is far too much of the "nothing beats a satisfied customer" routine. Even Chaney and Lewis, strong advocates of the church growth movement, are so alarmed as to warn that the success-at-all-costs syndrome must be resisted.[34]

Receptivity and the City

Church growth has as one of its basic tenets for success the principle that the location of church ministry must be determined by where that ministry succeeds. We must go only to places where our scientific and sociological data indicate that people will respond. According to church growth, "the Early Church allowed the numbers baptized to determine the direction and intensity of its missions . . . the New Testament Church went where men responded, believing this to be God's will."[35]

This prejudged response is based upon the principle of receptivity, or "good soil people." McGavran in his basic volume devotes an entire chapter to "The Receptivity of Men and Societies."[36] He claims that you can actually list the causes of fluctuation in response, and upon this calculation the entire strategy of world missions can be plotted. "Fitting method to receptivity" then becomes the primary task.

Many of the judgments are common sense judgments and do offer valuable guidance. McGavran recalls a visit to Mindanao in the Philippines where his host showed him a fairly new section with palm trees eight feet tall and suggested that new churches would grow there. He was making reference to the new population in that area as indicated by the young trees. It is new and exciting to be part of a recently planted community. Many mission boards have discovered that if you go in when the community is planted and before people settle into their routines and patterns, it is much easier to interest them in the new mission or church that has just been planted. But what do you do when a community is older? Desert it because the percentage and rate of productivity is smaller?

This emphasis on the "good soil people" suggests that God gets certain harvests ready; the church is to discern which harvests are ready and then send out workers accordingly (Luke 10:2). Here the movement seems to be based on a mixture of sociology and the kind of Calvinist theology that implies that some people are elected by God for salvation and some are not. In this instance I am pained both by the mechanics and the theology. This is not to suggest, however, that there is not some wisdom in being astute observers of human readiness. When Paul engaged in his Gentile ministry, he appears to have approached the "Godfearers" first, presumably on the assumption that they were more predisposed to what he had to share. Every experienced pastor has developed the "listening ear" approach, and that sixth sense that is alert to every opening. There are times when people are more open to us than at others. It is wise to have the "principle of strategic location" in mind; but it is too much to argue, as Tippett does, that Paul went to the Gentiles rather than to the Jews only because there was more willingness to respond.[37]

I become alarmed by the next step in the principle of strategic location—receptivity—"good soil people" approach. This step makes receptivity *dependent* on social and cultural factors. The natural conclusion is that if one can so accurately use sociological and anthropological tools to isolate the success factors, it is but a small step to the use of those same tools in manipulating and conditioning people to bring them from a state of resistance to a state of readiness.[38] The sovereignty of God and the place of the Holy Spirit in ministry are subjects that find little emphasis in this phase of the church growth material. The degree of "ripeness" may not be so obvious, and surely "ripeness" is not related to a mere technique of artificial insemination or stimulation.

There is a related negative to the wide extension of the receptivity principle. Surely the receptivity principle does have some validity in sensitizing one to the opportunity of ministry, but such a strong use of the principle as is found in the church growth movement easily leads to the neglect of the most needy. As in industry or strategizing for marketing, we are encouraged to vacate the less productive areas. This strong emphasis on the choice of target populations according to the criterion of success leads the church growth people to neglect the city with its economic mobility, changing neighborhoods, and racial mixture. The preference is for the suburbs, with its succeeding rings that mobility and economics establish. Here again the biblical concern for the dispossessed and powerless will be minimized, for the areas where such people live are not generally the most productive areas.

This is to say, in effect, that urban ministry is hopeless. This builds on the thesis so frequently heard these days from some sociologists and urbanologists who encourage a determined plan of abandonment of the cities of the Northeast, for instance, and a planned movement to more comfortable areas in the Sun Belt. The arguments are so very, very similar. This theme runs throughout so much of the church growth literature. The homogeneous principle contributes to it. Throughout the literature we are encouraged to place the church in and fashion its ministry to the natural shape of the community but then are told again and again that the community must have a homogeneous face in order for that church to succeed. The church growth institute does not appear to perceive multifaceted communities. One of the major concerns I have is the institute's seeming lack of understanding of what is characteristic of the cities across this country. I personally live in and serve a church in a portion of Chicago that is quite unlike the homogeneous unit that church growth wants. Judging from the constituency of the high school in our area, we would need to set up about fifty-two church units in order to create "comfortable" settings. Since this climate does not create ready receptivity, the principle would encourage us to move elsewhere with our efforts. I listened the other day to the principal of our Senn High

School talk about the difficulties of his work in trying to provide the atmosphere and different levels of opportunity necessary for working with such a diverse group of people. He compared it with more conventional high schools in homogeneous residential neighborhoods. But I did not hear the notes of despair or abandonment. I heard the sound of excitement at the privilege of bridging fragmentation and helping all to realize that they are part of the same human family. This is increasingly the pattern of our cities and the pattern of our world, and it is that pattern which church growth wants us to neglect. Not only does this sound like a call to abandon the city, but it also sounds like a methodology that may have had some basis in the tribal past but which is not geared "to guide us into the urban world of the future." [39]

I am aware that in some of his writings, McGavran does express concern for the city. There is a very fine statement in *How to Grow a Church* in which he suggests that cities need to remain great citadels of the church. I am afraid it is more of a passing kind of statement, however, when he suggests that "city people need Christ just as much as anybody else." [40] The major problem is that the philosophy and the methods are geared to nonurban areas, at least as we know them in the American cities. In many ways the church growth movement perpetuates a viewpoint heard long ago in which "studies of Protestant attendance disclose a maze of churchgoing patterns in the city, but the key to this maze is the search by middle-class people for socially homogeneous groupings, and the key to homogeneity is economic level." [41]

Those who make so much of finding a Bible context for every phase of the church growth movement might well remember that the church began in a city, Jerusalem, and spread from city to city across the Roman Empire. In spite of the many evils associated with the city, it is with a transformed city that the New Testament ends. Writers Shriver and Ostrom ask whether there is any hope for the city and respond affirmatively *if* the church in the city will maintain its place as a channel of grace. [42] It is impossible for the church to forget the city. It must be there as the presence of Christ and as the deed of Christ. The church will affirm the city. The church will be a peacemaker in the city and at the same time serve as a social critic in the city. This cannot be, however, if the church itself, as church growth would suggest that it should, remains the most segregated institution in the city. In this instance homogeneity must be cast aside. It is tragic when the neighborhood changes and other institutions in that neighborhood change while the church lags far behind. More and more as change comes to the city, several ethnic groups occupy the same neighborhood. We must indeed find ways for several ethnic groups to be together in the same church, serving as the body of Christ in that place. Negative social selectivity must disappear, and the churches must embrace social progress and practical unity.[43]

The church growth thesis is that this is difficult and impossible and cannot show the numerical increase that will be shown in more receptive, homogeneous areas. Yes, it is very difficult, but by the grace of God it is not impossible. The numerical gains will not look as good in church headquarters, but when did that become the final criterion of life and witness? It is true that some churches may lose their lives in the process, but Jesus had something to say about losing one's life.

Church growth people talk about the importance of the positive attitude and suggest that such a mental set has much to do with growth. The insistence on the principle of homogeneity causes people in the churches to view the city negatively, and, of course, if the city is viewed negatively, the church will shrink from the city. Jesus loved the city and wept over the city and likewise gave himself for its ultimate salvation. The church as the continuing incarnation and as the body of Christ is needed in the city.

The city remains the center of power and the hub of activity. At the moment there is some evidence that flight from the city in many instances is terminating and that "in-migration" is taking place. A survey of the neighborhood association in which I serve reveals that many of the houses have been purchased during the last four years by younger couples and families who have moved back into the city. Residential housing in the downtown area is at a premium. The church cannot have a negative attitude about the city at a time when there are some new positive attitudes. James D. Smart wrote a book on civil religion in which he contended that there has been a cultural subversion of the biblical faith.[44] To desert the city because the church wishes to work more comfortably in a more compatible homogeneous, receptive, "good growth" kind of setting is another kind of cultural subversion.

The church in the city is challenged not to retreat. Religious judicatories and national bodies are urged to do more than talk about the city. Instead of standing by and becoming angry when a city church cannot any longer be the chief contributor to denominational coffers, let the denomination join forces and cooperate in a new evangelistic thrust through that very church. In the cities we have previously followed two patterns with our church buildings. Either we have allowed a homogeneous group to hold on and keep others out until that group is too weak to make decisions, or we have encouraged others to flight and relocation so that a new homogeneous group can take over. The latter is certainly better than the former. But now let us focus on the discovery that God's family *is* heterogeneous, and let us positively pursue a heterogeneous direction when and where that is the pattern of the area in which a church is needed. Jacques Ellul calls us a city transfigured and believes that God is electing the city as an instrument of grace.[45] If God is in the city at all, let not the city be devoid of the church, no matter how difficult the church's ministry may be. Neither within the city nor anywhere else would I want anyone to be *forced* into a strange cultural pattern. At the same time, church growth does not sufficiently recognize emerging new social patterns or open itself to the new shapes and calls of God.

Ecumenical Posture

Church growth does not recognize any ecumenical posture. It warns against ecumenical concerns and suggests that ecumenism drains away energies and further takes away the sharp edge of competitiveness which "beats the other guy" and leads to success. They believe that one cannot evangelize and call for the unity of the body of Christ all at the same time. In "A Personal Message from the Authors," McGavran and Arn call ecumenicity one of the major nongrowth factors during the 1960s.[46] An ecumenical spirit is said to cause evangelism to be nonexistent since it assumes that everyone is already Christian. That in itself is a caricature that does not accurately describe the ecumenical movement as I have known it in three urban areas. Ecumenicity was encouraged precisely because the pressures of a non-Christian world were experienced and Christians needed the insights and encouragements of one another. Nor has it been my experience, as church growth charges, that ecumenicity is responsible for moral relativism and "whatever anyone thinks is right, is right for them." Some of the most serious ethical and theological thought in which I have ever been involved has been under the aegis of ecumenical groups who were truly struggling for integrity in the biblical and theological understandings of our world and an appropriate life-style in it. If there is any relativism, it is in the view of discipling, argued and promoted by church growth, which suggests that through people movements and whatever process, you "get them in" and then hope that you can begin to teach them the difference it ought to make after they are captured.

Much correspondence has gone back and forth between the School of World Mission at Fuller Seminary and the World Council of Churches on these matters.[47] I am prone to believe that there is a much easier escape from the gospel's demands which does not require the painful crossing of barriers than one which makes a point that there are barriers. The interesting observation must be that it is the School of World Mission and Institute of Church Growth that provides the easy way and not the World Council. It is a peculiar fact, as John H. Yoder suggests, that the church growth people accuse the ecumenical stance of the World Council of Churches as "inclusivism" when in missionary method this "inclusivism" is a major plank in the McGavran thesis.[48] Prior to 1968 McGavran was much more friendly to the ecumenical position. One wonders whether the clashes of viewpoint and attack did not become more stringent because of some change in political fortunes with the World Council.

Allan H. Howe in a paper called "The Church: Its Growth and Mission" talks about unity in Christ as one of the givens in the Christian way and requires "that in the life of the church as the body of Christ the visible, corporate presence of the one new humanity in Him becomes manifest to the world. . . ."[49] The wholeness of the church as the people of God is not something to be achieved; it is the biblical given. One cannot ignore that given as though it were unimportant, nor can one ignore it in the interest of numbers. A call unto God is a call unto one another in the church, and every believer has to reckon with that. Ecumenism is not simply a "cozy feeling" that delights in Christian fellowship for its own sake. Ecumenism would take risks to achieve a unity for the purpose of mission, a mission addressed to both united witness and united service in the world in order that the world may come to believe. The church does not exist for the church's sake. The church exists for the world's sake. Neither is ecumenism a quest for one bloated superchurch, believing nothing, with bureaucracy and bigness and a loss of our several traditions. It is a recognition that humankind is incurably diverse, but because of its common confession of Jesus Christ as Lord and Savior, it seeks to be a genuine community and seeks to enjoy the fullness of that community as the family of God. The goal of true ecumenism is unity-in-creative-diversity, and the unity begins with an identity with Jesus Christ and his call of the kingdom. The form and expression of this unity is at least threefold, including social, theological, and spiritual dimensions. It is perhaps in the social dimension where churches extend themselves in common outreach to a suffering humanity that church growth people part company, for, as expressed elsewhere, they are frightened by the social dimension of the gospel.

We, therefore, need to get some perspective. Once, after the Reformation when it became obvious that numerous denominations were going to be the order of the day, these denominations vied with one another in their evangelistic outreach. This was increasingly true in the expanding field of world (foreign) missions. Denominational Protestantism coincided with and accompanied the colonial expansion of Western Europe around the globe. The 1800s saw the rapid expansion of Christianity into many parts of the world. By the time of the twentieth century, however, our rival missions and missionaries began to collide with one another, and confusion and competition began to affect the basic character of Christian mission. Increasingly it was discovered that the world would not well receive a Christian witness from fragmented and competing churches. A young Japanese, for example, attempting to make a Christian commitment, cried out in the splintered anguish of his soul: "My father is a member of the Holiness church, my mother is a Methodist, my brother is an Episcopalian, my wife is a Baptist, I am a Presbyterian, one cousin is an American Baptist, and one is a Southern Baptist. Why are there such divisions in the family of God?'' If church growth is concerned about the response of people, it must be aware of the agony of being caught in the crush of 250 Protestant denominations, the numerous Catholic groups—Roman, with its competing religious orders which are almost denominations in themselves—and Eastern Orthodox with about 20 subdivisions.

In the multiethnic, multilanguage church of which I am a part, we have discovered that when a Christian from an Indian village meets a Christian from a Chinese farm, European factory, or Japanese city, differences of denomination are of no essential importance and the Christian fellowship minimizes the differences of language, culture, and color. What counts most is the primary fact that each believes in the one God and Father of Jesus Christ, that the same gospel is confessed, and that baptism in the Holy Spirit is shared. Whoever does the will of God is brother, sister, relative.

Church growth advocates are mostly from very conservative denominations. Although church growth itself minimizes ecumenicity, many of these conservative denominations have learned to coordinate their mission and witness in international missions. For a long time now on the mission fields of the world, there has been a growing sense of oneness in the family of God. It is something to behold, to view the cooperation between once feuding groups in Central and South America. It has likewise been challenging to see properties turned over to indigenous missions and a multiple increase in the number of converts per dollar expended.

But here at home we have been slow to learn. Some of the church's difficulty in the city may be because one God has been verbalized but one church and one mission have been far from us until slowly we are discovering that the price of a divided Christendom is a weak, demoralized, and nullified mission. An insistence upon segregated cultures is fragmenting enough. The insistence upon a fragmented church is a further contribution to a fragmented community.

Church growth people often refer to the 1960s and blame some of the problems of the decade on the ecumenical church. We might well remember that secular humanism hit us and tended to usurp Christianity as humankind's religion and we were too scattered in our isolation to bear much witness against it. Holocaust developed in our society, demoralization set in, and urban crisis interrupted our peaceful dream of heaven. The church is called to confession because we surely carried some responsibility for the explosions. The churches were not playing the same tune and often had erected walls so as to drown out the tunes of one another and the wounds of a waiting world needing our kind of musical therapy. We are in a similar kind of situation again. On a global scale we are confronted with all of the needs of a Third World people, and on a national scene we have growing indications of a non-caring attitude about the millions of people who have been victims of our kind of society. Church growth people ask us to continue on with our institutional building, refusing as the larger family of God either to contemplate the problems together or to address them.

Contrary to the contentions of McGavran and others, ecumenists are not calling for a bland doctrinal confession where everything is reduced to the lowest common denominator. Form is, of course, negotiable, but the loving community of one human being for another resulting from a personal and corporate identity with Jesus Christ is not. The call is for a church that is experience-centered and action-oriented, not one or the other. The Christian community began with an event in history, God in Christ. It was that sense of Christocentric community which enabled the church to survive a succession of severe crises. The place for us to begin is not with some watered-down formulation of propositional truths. The place to begin is with Jesus Christ, experientially encountered in faith. When we have met Christ (and even some members of the church today may find this to be a new experience, thus we need McGavran's E-0 evangelism), then we are prepared to venture to shape the oneness to which God has called us for the sake of bearing witness in the world.

But an experience-centered church will be an action-directed church. Jesus tells a parable in which a father approached his elder son and said to him, "Son, go out and work in the vineyard," and the son replied, "Yes," but never did go. The father approached a second son and made the same request. The second son said, "No," but later regretted it and went (Matthew 21:28-31). Believing is a faith relationship actively expressed.

These experience-centered, action-directed people are joined together as the people of God, and the people of God have a united identity and make a positive gospel proclamation. There are many urban areas where this proclamation can best be done in an ecumenical style. I remember those earlier days of ministry when I did not know what the word "ecumenical" meant and had never encountered the ecumenical movement under some banner *per se*. Yet at the same time, we discovered the values of churches in a community working together in order to take a common religious census and project a common strategy of evangelism. We recognized collectively that what we had to contribute was not a call to a nebulous belief in God in general but a call that asked people to decide in particular about Jesus Christ as the personification of redemptive experience with God.

I am encouraged that some of the more recent church growth people are beginning to recognize some substance to the ecumenical call. Charles Mylander recognizes the value of intercongregational activities and agrees that "any wholesome activity that shows cooperation with Christians from other homogeneous churches is desirable.''[50] I am sorry that there is such strong stress on ''homogeneous,'' but it is encouraging to see intercongregational cooperation activity raised as a vital issue in church growth material.

Where shall we go to search for guides to this unity? Well, of course, Christ is our uniting person and the Bible is our uniting source. But I would also like to suggest that we turn once again for a serious look at the documents that came from Vatican II. There are so many ''evangelical'' Christians these days within the Roman Catholic church. If those ''Romans'' and concerned Protestants within a community got together, a tremendous concerted effort could be made on any particular geographical area. Three of the decrees in particular from Vatican II will be of help. The ''Decree on Ecumenism'' makes it very clear that there is no unity outside of HIS unity. Therefore, the decree is, in contrast to the Roman Catholic church's traditional call for unity, a call to return to Christ; it is a call to renewal. The ''Dogmatic Constitution on the Church'' has as its themes the people of God concept, the importance of laity, the pilgrim church, the priesthood of the believer, and the covenant community. The third decree ''The Dogmatic Constitution on Revelation,'' affirms God as the source of revelation through both Scripture and tradition, a tradition that must be tested by the biblical witness. The place of the Scripture receives strategic stress within the life of the church. Rather than fight the ecumenical spirit, we might well be called to the possible realization that materials are at hand for helping us to realize the unity that is such a vital part of our Lord's last will and testament in John's Gospel (chapters 13–17). If such unity is desired by our Lord, and I believe that it is, then that unity will also contribute to the evangelization of the world, which I also believe to be our Lord's will. As such, the church neither has to decide to be separated nor to choose between ''evangelizing the world'' and ''seeking to make the world a better place.''[51]

Congregational Style, the Clergyperson, and Preaching

Although this phase of the evaluation centers on the pastor, it involves two aspects in particular: (1) polity and administration and (2) worship. Therefore, we put them together as captioned in the above manner.

At the same time, the reader should recognize that the author values his free-church tradition and those parts in that tradition that come from an Anabaptist heritage. The evaluation is in some sense a response to attacks upon that heritage through church growth viewpoints on the three items in the caption. The concern centers on the pastor, his or her style and task, and his or her relationship to the congregation in the accomplishment of his or her task.

Wagner suggests that *"Vital Sign Number One of a healthy, growing church is a pastor who is a possibility thinker and whose dynamic leadership has been used to catalyze the entire church into action for growth.''* [52] Since the pastor is the catalytic factor for growth in a local church, he or she is encouraged ''not to be afraid of power.'' Furthermore, one is encouraged to ''do what one has to do'' to cause the people to think of their pastor as the greatest, i.e., build a kind of personality cult. To enhance one's leadership, the pastor should secure a staff that has no interest in doing the things the senior pastor does, thus making pastoral authority all the more complete. One should be the company commander who gets one's orders from the ''commander in chief'' and do away with the plurality of committees who dilute the power. The leader must be the leader, the executive head if you will, directing all activities. Wagner suggests that a pastor may appear to be a dictator to outsiders, but ''to the people of the church, his decisions are their decisions.'' [53] The people of the church should realize that ''almost as if he had a sixth sense, he knows how to lead the church where the people want to go. . . .'' [54] In order to secure this authority and this allegiance, Wagner quotes approvingly that the pastor should ''scratch 'em where they itch.''

The pattern that is suggested for accomplishing this kind of leadership is a church with a one-board administrative structure, with the pastor serving as the president of the corporation. In order to clinch the authority, Hebrews 13:17 is given as a legitimizing proof text: ''Obey your leaders and follow their orders. They watch over your souls without resting, since they must give to God an account of their service. If you obey them, they will do their work gladly; if not, they will do it with sadness, and that would be of no help to you'' (TEV). [55] Once the pastor has been given this kind of authority, he or she then is charged with the full responsibility of the church's success or failure. According to Wagner: ''Church people . . . realize . . . that if a person accepts the responsibility of being the pastor of a church, he accepts the primary responsibility for its growth or decline just as much as an airplane pilot accepts responsibility for keeping his plane in the air.'' [56]

In order to enhance the stewardship and authority of this administrative autocrat, the pastor should not get too involved in the ''pastoral'' side of the church's life. Part of Wagner's emphasis is an attempt to correct a condition that we all recognize—the congregation employs the pastor and expects him or her to do the work of the church. The pattern of the membership as spectators rather than participants is familiar to us all. This is not the major emphasis, however. In the church growth plan, rather than sharing ''pastoral'' duties with church members, the pastor as administrative leader is encouraged to abdicate all such responsibilities. Wagner defines the gift of pastor as ''the special ability that God gives to certain members of the Body of Christ to assume a long-term personal responsibility for the spiritual welfare of a group of believers.'' [57] If the pastor is too much involved in the shepherding of one's people, it will consume one's time and impede the growth of the church.

As a pastor, I am well aware of the tension between shepherding and evangelizing. I would likewise agree that no matter how large or small the congregation is, there is never an end to the pastoral need. However, to suggest that the pastoral gift is not needed because that task can be left to others is to contribute to a condition that is all too frequent, i.e., the lack of pastoral attention to the wounds and bruises of people. Everybody has a story, and attention is needed. "I am not employed to hold hands," already is too frequently heard from pastors who are afraid to get involved in the lives of people. There is something wrong with a program that does not allow the pastor to be a shepherd. Using another image, I must agree that far too many of us pastors relate to the membership as policyholders whom we must service and too few of us are agents out in the field selling more insurance. But to neglect the opportunity of pastoral care and to suggest that this is an outmoded expectation of the pastor is to give a priority to numbers, which easily makes the church something less than the church.

The next step is to suggest that preaching is not an important task either as compared to the administration of an institutional growth plan. This is exactly what Wagner advocates. He wants us to be neither preachers nor pastors and suggests that "while preachers tend to draw the attention of others to themselves, pastors tend to pour out their attention on others."[58] The net effect of this suggestion is to minimize the pastor's role as worship leader.

I do agree that the pastor is the key to church growth, and experience indicates that if the pastor neglects an area, that area is likely to stay neglected. I do likewise agree that others in the congregation need the pastoral gift. There is true health in a congregation in which all the members are the "ministers of the church," caring for one another. However if laity can perform in all of the other areas of the church's life, they can likewise assume responsibility in church growth. To place all of the growth responsibility on the pastor's shoulders and to neglect the traditional ministries of the pastoral role is equally incorrect and commits the same error in another direction. There is something scheming, yes, demonic, in the suggestion that it is more important to be dreaming big dreams about building cathedrals than to be doing pastoral work.[59] I readily accept the indictment that we have not been sufficiently intentional about growth. I cannot accept the thesis that if one truly wishes to be a pastor, the church cannot grow. Wagner wishes to refashion all systems of ministerial training in order to focus on building bigger churches. But are huge churches what we really want to grow, and is the bigness of the institution the primary goal? Evangelizing and winning the masses is a desired goal. This might

better be done and the church might better be the church through a multiplication of pastor-led fellowships of smaller size rather than the continual
creation of huge numbers of people with the accompanying real estate
holdings. Our seminary and divinity school institutions do need curriculum
changes. The student needs more pastoral skills, however, and not less.
Too many students and veteran pastors already feel that they have not
succeeded because they are not pastors of "big" churches. I would like the
"big church" syndrome to become less the goal rather than more.

This, as I see it, distorted view of the pastor's task is somewhat related
to church growth's denigration of the congregational form of church government. I must admit that my defenses are up when church growth people
tell me that "for growing churches the congregational form of government
is like a millstone around its neck."[60] According to Wagner, a congregational form of polity is counterproductive to growth and the pastor must
find some way to subvert its nature.[61] Is it by analogy to be argued that
since there are inefficiencies in democracies, it is better to build a fascist
system with dictators? Congregational polity is surely not *the* biblical shape
of the church. Elements of every form of polity are to be found in the New
Testament. I fear, however, that the numbers goal has blinded church
growth advocates to other very good and necessary qualities of church life.
That the numbers goal succeeds is not a sufficient argument for overlooking
those elements which make the church the church!

In this regard as relates to both pastor and congregation, one additional
element needs to be scrutinized. My study of the church growth movement
leads me to the continuing impression that the preaching ministry is minimized. McGavran and Arn quote with approval a Puerto Rican pastor's
appraisal, "My sermons have little to do with it."[62] Wagner further minimizes preaching with his statement that "proclaiming the gospel does not
particularly require a spiritual gift."[63] Although these statements are intended in context to throw the spotlight upon the importance of the small-
group, "upper room" principle of church organization, they represent more
of the continuing attitude that if you just use the right mechanical technique,
everything will come up roses.

In the church growth movement we have a good thing gone wrong,
namely, the goal has become more important than the motivation, and this
is largely due to the loss of biblical, theological, and historical perspective.
Church growth as a technique to be learned basically ignores the sense of
"call" that has been so much a part of ministry. It also fails to recognize
the tasks of the "called" one as they are rooted in biblical history.

The biblical tradition of "call" is generally traced to such backgrounds
as that of Moses (Exodus 3), Isaiah (Isaiah 6), or Jeremiah (Jeremiah 1).
In each instance there is something of the threefold vision of God (Isaiah
6:1), of ourselves (Isaiah 6:5), and of a needy world (Isaiah 6:8f.).[64] This

call is definitely related to the religious institution and that religious institution had at least three kinds of functionaries—priests, prophets, and wise men. Three of the tasks that the techniques of church growth minimize are inherent in the roles of those functionaries: proclamation (prophets), interpretation (priests), and application (wise men). Indeed, we would not have the biblical material from the Old Testament except as it was transmitted by these three. The Torah came to us as the gift of the priests, prophetic material as the contribution of the prophets, and the Writings (commonly known as wisdom literature) from the wise men.

If these were the tasks, then the style was the familiar style of the suffering servant. This pattern of ministry is to be traced to Moses who mediated between God and Israel. It was Moses who exposed himself to the voice of God in Israel's place and then spoke to Israel in God's place (Deuteronomy 5:27). Moses vicariously represented the people in meetings with God. He had to interpret the anger of God after the sin of the worship of the golden calf. Forty days and forty nights were spent in intercessory work (Deuteronomy 9:18f., 26f.; cf. Exodus 32:32). On account of the sins of his people, Moses was not allowed to enter the Promised Land (Deuteronomy 1:37; 4:21), and he died outside of Israel. The renewal of the covenant takes place through Moses (Exodus 32:32; 34:9), and he offers to give his life in place of those whose disobedience had called for the loss of life. The Suffering Servant ministry of Jesus (Mark 10:45) has its roots in the Mosaic period and is transmitted to Jesus through the Suffering Servant pattern of Isaiah 40–66. The ministry of Jesus pulled together the Old Testament patterns of ministry, and Jesus embodied the functions of prophet, priest, and wise man. That pattern of ministry was never repudiated, as underscored by Paul in various places (e.g., Romans 10; Philippians 2). This does not mean that ministers are to allow themselves to become "go-fers" and thus be distracted from the substantive aspects of ministry. We are in agreement here with the church growth people. It is on the question of where the priorities are to be in the use of the time afforded that we find disagreement. Besieged by the impossible, too many ministers do develop a "martyr complex" and lose their energies. The resultant ineffectiveness becomes evident not only in numerical growth patterns but in other aspects of ministry. This, however, serves to bring the focus back to the ground pattern of ministry. The word "martyr" has no initial relationship to an abused person. The martyr is someone who has been witness to something and now shares responsibility to bear a witness to that which has been seen or heard. One hears this witness as a herald *(keryx)*, one who proclaims that to which and about which one has been witness. The pastor must not be swamped by "having to do everything." At the same time, caution is advised in minimizing the core functions that have been the substance of the minister's pattern from earlier generations.

Being a technical specialist is of little value if there is no life and substance to deliver. The pastor does not have to relinquish his or her leadership in a caring fellowship and in quality worship and become merely an administrative numbers specialist.

I am bothered by the frequent church growth presentation of the pastor as someone who must stand "over and against" the community of faith of which he or she is a part. The pastor is not "over and against" but "part of" the community. We need to think more frequently of the communal setting of the minister's task. Who the pastor is will be defined in terms of his or her relationship to the entire community. This is especially true in terms of the "sacrament" of preaching, a task minimized by church growth. Thus, we will use the preaching task to illustrate the necessity of the pastor's standing "within" the community rather than "over and against" it. The renewal of the preaching ministry is to be found in the discovery of its communal character. Preaching involves not only the preacher but also the hearers. When the preacher sits down to work on a message, he or she strives to be aware both of the congregation and of self. The task is to visualize the congregation with its variety of stories and needs. This cannot be done unless the pastor has been in "pastoral" touch with his or her people. Although church growth people believe they have a system that is transportable from place to place and works everywhere, programs and sermons are not transportable. There is not some "general" message that suits everywhere. In the actual situation congregation and minister make the sermon a mutual exploration by both parties. Together we are engaged in creating a covenant setting and atmosphere that make it possible for God to do something. The responsibilities of the laity in the exchange are indeed the same as those of the preacher, for the preacher is not a performer putting on a show that laity, as a group of spectators, enjoys. Parenthetically, I must admit that the "performer" technique in a "religious variety show setting" is sometimes a more successful way of getting a larger attendance ("audience").

I heard about a wise congregation a short time ago. The church had been through a terrible turmoil and seemed not to be united. The new minister's sermons just did not seem to click. When some wished only to grumble, a wiser group said, "No, let's help him preach." Because they began bringing to the worship hour their preparation of prayer and deliberate reflection on the meaning of events in their lives that week, and poured into the atmosphere the fruits of small-group discussion about the meaning of life, they helped a congregation both to "come alive" and, with and through their pastor, to become as a church one of the outstanding voices for God in that area. The pastor now speaks with the community rather than either over and against it, merely to it, or from outside of it.

The minister preaches *his* or *her* sermon in order that other sermons may be brought into being in the congregation, sermons that will be the joint products of both *his* or *her* and the congregation's efforts. Having put the thought of the congregation into orbit, i.e., having activated the thought of the congregation into some form that might travel with the members, then the minister's sermon—once it is preached—has served its purpose and is destined for oblivion. It continues to live only insofar as it lives in the fruit of the meeting of meaning between the minister and the congregation.

Too often we have thought of the dialogue sermon as two people, probably the pastor and a lay person, sharing the platform together. There is a place for that as a novel and infrequent experience. But real preaching is dialogue in that the sermon grows out of the needs and experiences of the covenant community itself. Thus, the secret is in growing the covenant community. Both pastoral and preaching gifts *are* needed. Because the listener can sense that the preacher is empathetically seeking to travel the same road and engage in the same quest, he or she can be gripped by the formation of that same message within himself or herself. The preacher approaches his or her community, not so much to proclaim an answer as to witness to a person, Jesus Christ; and Christ speaks. Preaching definitely is not the exclusive responsibility of the preacher alone. Perhaps if church growth people could give some study time to the nature of preaching, they would rediscover preaching as a valid element which strengthens the community in its ministry of reaching out. Minister and congregation together will recognize that "preaching is an encounter involving not only content but relationship, not only ideas but action, not only logic but emotion, not only understanding but commitment."[65]

In preaching as well as in everything else in the life of the church, the pastor must get off center stage and put the spotlight where it belongs, pinpointing the mutual responsibility of the entire people of God. We are concerned about the proclamation of the church and not the proclamation of the pastor. At the same time, the spotlight cannot be put where it belongs unless the pastor stands with the community as a wounded healer. Free-church people who have long had the tradition of the priesthood of *all* believers do not wish to relegate authority in any area to any one person.

Perhaps the primary key to our discussion is the "confessional stance." The pastor is an individual, a fellow pilgrim, not a superperson, and the people will not expect him or her to be such a superperson unless he or she has assumed that air. Preaching cannot be communal unless it is confessional.

Furthermore, church growth would minimize neither preaching nor the pastoral stance that contributes to preaching if its sacramental nature were contemplated. There is a certain mystery about preaching. Things are heard that we did not say. Things weak and feeble sometimes assume proportions of strength within a life or lives that we never dreamed possible. The preacher discovers that the words he or she was speaking became the means of preparing the way for God's speaking, the mystery being that through and by means of these words "the everlasting Gospel is contemporized, and not only contemporized but individualized, and not merely individualized but actualized."[66] It is this mystery that causes us to speak about the "sacramental nature of preaching." If we have not experienced the mystery, we have not preached. We need not be afraid of the word "sacrament." It was first used of the oath of office Roman soldiers took as they entered the military service. They gave a *sacramentum* of loyalty as they entered military life. Gradually *sacramentum* was applied to the entrance itself. Thus, baptism, the entrance rite into the Christian church, became a sacrament, indicating not only the rite, but also the rights, privileges, and blessings that went with it. It became a sign and a vehicle of something else.

Since there is no true preaching just as there is no true baptism and no true Eucharist unless God is at work in it through the Holy Spirit, so as baptism and Eucharist have a sacramental aspect, likewise does preaching. If the recipient is willing, both preaching (Word) and Communion may mediate God's presence with his responsive people. Preaching as sacrament, thus, has in mind the double nature of "word." God the living Word comes uniquely through these human words in a way the speaker of them does not understand. As in the Supper (a memorial), we remember what God did in Christ, but as the recollection is brought before us, what God *did* in Christ, God is now *doing* so that there is a *re-presentation;* as the words are being spoken, the deed is again being done. "This contemporaneity of what has long since happened, this actuality in the present of what is also remembered in the past,"[67] this *wasness* that becomes *isness,* this *pastness* that becomes *presentness*—this is sacrament and this is preaching. If the Lord's Supper is the visible Word, then the proclaimed word of preaching may be the audible Word. Preaching becomes event, and new response is required as people experience human need and God's grace, and are faced with the necessity of decision.

Therefore, to minimize the pastoral stance is to minimize preaching. To minimize preaching is to rob the faith community of that energizing force that would cause it to want to go out and win the world. To eradicate congregational significance is to lose the very sense of community that the church growth movement pleads for in other instances.

4

A Positive Ministry for Growth

The church growth movement seeks to give a sense of confidence back to the church. It is unapologetic in having the native faith and courage to believe that the church should confront those outside its doors. The Great Commission is taken seriously, and it is openly recognized that we have been less than faithful in expecting little more than biological growth, the reception of the children of members into the church. We have become part of a tired church and know little about "the positive spirit." Most of us in main-line and liberal churches have used a "remnant theology" for so long as a justification for our failure to grow that we have lost the motivation to be Christ's evangels.

In our defensive posturing we have been guilty of faulty logic. I agree, for instance, with the major thrust of Robert K. Hudnut's little book *Church Growth Is Not the Point,* but one cannot, as he does, see it as a good sign that people are leaving the churches. Nor would I, as does he, rationalize that "loss of growth in statistics has often meant increase in growth in the Gospel." [1] It is debatable as to whether those we have left really are the faithful remnant.

I am in the position of greatly favoring the characteristics of growing churches. A growth goal consciousness, the recognition that laity are the ministers of God, priority for evangelism, some appreciation for homogeneous reality, attention to discipleship, a search to recognize our gifts and appreciation for the body of Christ—all of these are positive thrusts with both biblical and practical support. I am grateful to church growth advocates for drawing the outline.

I can even recognize that there is some validity at the point where I am most critical of the movement—the thesis of homogeneity. It is when it is made the norm and carried to such extremes that validity is lost. The old "melting pot" theory is not satisfactory. This suggests that everyone should lose one's peculiar identity. To do so is to require far less than the distinctiveness with which God made us. We need to retain our individual strengths and find some way of bridging the gaps in order to contribute these strengths to one another. An assimilated model, usually of the Anglo-conforming variety, will not do. The mosaic model of dwelling side by side with no touching and no cross-flavoring is likewise insufficient. As uneuphonious as it sounds, perhaps the symbol reportedly to be attributed to Andrew Greely, the "stew pot" vision, does have some value. Each ingredient adds its own characteristic flavor to the whole but in some distinctive way also maintains its identity. One does not have to lose individuality or identity in order to be part of the "new creation, the new humanity," in Christ.

The push for the required characteristics for growth expounded by the church growth movement may well serve to jolt us from a timidity that blocks any efforts at all in planting churches and growth. Along with all of the institutional-centered committees, perhaps we will, because of the church growth movement, begin to find a place for unapologetically sharing our faith from the experiential point of view. Perhaps we will regain the confidence openly to help individuals and communities deal with life in terms of its ultimate meaning.

I strongly favor many of the ingredients of the movement and will seek further to implement them by my own ministry. But it is the fact that it is a "movement," blindly charging ahead through its own momentum, which brings me fear. Elements that might have served as correctives are now "the truths." It is "the truths," or "the steps," to successful growth that constitute the new heresy. As so often happens when people become happy with what they have found, a sense of proportion has been lost. Primary elements of the church have become secondary. The right tool, it is believed, will fix anything. The result has been a literalistic and allegorical searching of the Scripture to support "the system." The heightened result is the quotation of Scripture to support homogeneity, done in a way that does not have the integrity of consistency with the whole gospel. The failure of social concern represents far less than Jesus himself presented as a test of kingdom citizenship. "Church" as institution assumes size far larger than the kingdom of God of which it is a part. The biblical journey from Babel to the New Jerusalem is forgotten, and urban ministry is doomed. The sin of ecumenical fragmentation is affirmed. The distinctive role of the pastor as a shepherding person has been traded for that of the secular corporate executive. The real danger is that these tenets may be emblematic of a movement that has success more than substance as its driving motivation. The problem is that it obviously succeeds. If one tailors the church to identify with its culture and engages in the pseudo-gospel of possibility thinking, promising to assuage guilt with a minimum of pain and connecting that with marketing techniques, there will be success. The problem is that there is a descending similarity to the church.

A Confessional Stance

Any ministry, including a ministry for growth, must first be tested within a confessional stance. In recent years, my own denomination has gone through various organizational patterns of operation. These efforts finally culminated in SCOR (Study Commission on Reorganization). Designs were drawn to create the highest efficiency and those designs have been adopted. A deficiency in the process was that we asked far more "organizational" questions than we did "confession of faith" questions. Organizational experts outside of the church had a large hand in building the organizational skeleton for the church. Now, after the fact, we are struggling to ask the theological and confession- of-faith questions. Church growth has not sufficiently asked the theological questions. Learnings from sociology have at times been more dominant than testings by confessions of faith. One wonders whether the "system" has not outvoiced the confession. The system has not been often enough and seriously enough tested by the "center that holds."

We do not know from day to day what the shape of the church ought to be for tomorrow. Neither do we know what techniques and methods will be best. We do know that no system is *the* biblical system. We do know that the church must be the venturing pilgrim church, filled with Christ's Spirit to accept whatever shape the day demands. In keeping with the confessional center, the church will be experience-centered and action-directed. The people of God will gather and share support, nurture, and strength for one another. But they will also scatter and share that life in presence and deed. The motivation, as the centering confession demands, will be for God's sake and for a world in need, rather than for "building bigger and better churches."

A Perspective for Ministry

This brings us full circle again to the emphasis with which chapter 3 was closed, attention to the role of the pastor and congregation in ministry. Church growth has many positive expressions about lay people serving as the ministers of the church. But then when the role of the pastor is presented, the picture does not mesh well. The pastor calls the shots and the lay people do the work, but it turns out to be primarily the work of recruiting yeoman.

A perspective on ministry, however, begins with the people and not with the pastor. At baptism every member of the church is ordained to ministry. These people of God are the priesthood of 1 Peter 2:9. The work of the pastor grows out of the ministry of the people of God. The pastor may be a representative of or extension of the ministry of the people of God. The people are the base and the pastor is the extension. We must not reverse the pattern so that the pastor is the base and the people are the extension. There is no conduit that runs from God through minister to people. Jesus Christ is the chief minister, and the people are an extension of his ministry. As the people of God arise from Christ's ministry, so the ordained minister in turn arises from the people of God. Extend this to a larger polity of a more episcopal type, and it means that the people of God direct the bishop rather than the bishop directing the people of God.

The epitome of all descriptions of ministry, of course, is the Suffering Servant description to be found in Isaiah 52–53. Isaiah 53:11 suggests that the righteous servant is to make many righteous. Thereupon, in Isaiah 54:17, the plural "servants" is used for the first time to describe the seed of Zion or the seed of the Servant: " . . . This is the heritage of the *servants* of the Lord . . ." (italics added). The pattern of ministry described for the Suffering Servant thus becomes the pattern of ministry for the *servants* (plural), the little servants who are schooled in the discipline of the Chief Servant, a discipline suggested by the third servant poem (Isaiah 50:4) and again in Isaiah 54:13.

Continuing emphasis on the messianic pattern of ministry is underscored by the book of Ephesians, which provides continuity with the Suffering Servant-messianic pattern by suggesting that the church is the continuing incarnation. As God became incarnate in particular fashion in Jesus Christ, so in the church he continues the incarnation. The church is not Christ's body unless it becomes "incarnate," too. This means that the church will share humankind's real spiritual as well as humankind's physical condition, even as did Jesus. That body will go beyond its own circle and share in humankind's wounds. Whatever pattern of ministry was appropriate for the first and major prototype of incarnation is applicable for the continuing incarnation. Since Christ is the pattern, the nature of ministry is automatically set—teaching, reconciling, healing, and serving. Ministry is always by the people. The entire body is the priest, and every individual within the body is a ministering priest who contributes to the priestly nature and function of the corporate whole. As an extension or representative of that ministry, the pastor will have the same characteristics and functions, although often in an "enabling" way.

Since the ministry of the church is the ministry of the whole church, of all of the people of God, it is appropriate that the ordained minister give the people guidance for recruiting persons into the church body and guidance for training and motivating persons as part of that body. A large amount of time must be spent, however, in servicing and training the ministers of the body. It is appropriate that much of the ordained person's "ministry is in the church, and it is sustained as the essential gift of God to the church in order that the ministry of the church to the world may be exercised."[2] Since the ordained person is concerned to help bring this ministering people of God into being, he or she most naturally must give himself or herself to church growth. A matter of proportionate emphasis is involved, however, because much of the ordained minister's time and effort must be spent in modeling ministry. The character of such ministry may be aided by a clue from the pattern given in the high priestly prayer of John 17, a ministry of *holiness* (17:15) or *being* something; a ministry of *mission* (17:18), not as a pietistic "within you" but as "in the midst"; a ministry possessed of *unity* (17:10, 20-21); and a ministry involving *glory* (17:24) for God, not for self.

"All the congregation as ministers" thus speaks of a general ministry of which the pastor is a representative minister. All are, rightly so, involved in the evangelistic and growth aspects. This shared task means that the paid staff minister will seek to maintain a sense of balance. The pastoral function will provide the context and perspective for the recruitment function. What is being attempted here is to develop a sense of perspective. Church growth is to be a focused goal, but it is not the only or the major goal, as so much of the technical literature of church growth might suggest.

Modeling Ministry

The biblical dimensions of growth are both inward and outward.[3] Therefore, the pastor must search for a style of ministry that will help to bring about that balance. Carnegie Samuel Calian has delineated eight distinguishable styles of ministry for the pastor. Briefly delineated, the eight are: (1) the servant-shepherd, the selfless servant who serves as "loving elder and parent to the congregation"; (2) the politician-prophet, the out-front minister dealing with issues in community context; (3) the preacher-teacher, the pastor who takes seriously the pulpit desk responsibilities of inspiration and information (teaching); (4) the evangelist-charismatic, providing a dimension of enthusiasm and warmth; (5) the pragmatist-promoter, the success syndrome in the "power of positive thinking" style; (6) the manager-enabler, management by objectives with planned management and forecasting; (7) the liturgist-celebrant, involving the consciousness that our chief end is to worship and glorify God; (8) the specialized ministries, mainly ministries in the counseling areas.[4]

There are three areas where most of us in main-line churches need improvement: evangelist-charismatic, pragmatist-promoter, and manager-enabler. We do need to know what we are trying to do and where we need to go. The church growth people have been very helpful about that, and we need to listen. If the paid staff person who has the opportunity to provide leadership in goal setting does not, then who will? We are engaged in the most important venture in human existence and are often so terribly sloppy and indefinite in the way we go about it. The church has allowed very cumbersome machinery to develop, and it probably is true that the church as an institution could be operated with only one-tenth of the committees we usually have.[5] Enthusiasm, pragmatism, and management skills are not bad qualities to have. But as we seek to develop these qualities, they must be set within the larger theological context of what the church and her ministry are all about. In the name of efficiency and numbers we cannot allow ourselves to forget that the church is more than business! The glamour of a Robert Schuller and his huge success cannot be allowed to bring an easy acceptance of culture. The difficult part of ministry is that we often must model the person who is in a cross fire between "techniques that win" and the essential necessity of taking the road and paying the price of traveling counterculture. The only success that is likely to produce is a cross, and we are right back at the Suffering Servant model again.

The model is one of faithfulness rather than success! But we can be more successful in our faithfulness if laity becomes so much a part of ministry that it "overcome[s] the temptation to crush the ecclesiastical leader every time a decision, act, or program runs contrary to expectations or vested interests."[6] One cannot lead if every step must have approval or consensus. At the same time, the leader will possess the humility of both shared ownership and personal accountability. Pastor and people must be willing to pay a price. Faith will not be viewed as a cautious life insurance policy, and conversion will be viewed as a direction rather than "entrance into a safe harbor."[7] Church growth wants the pastor to be an administrator; seminaries want the pastor to be the theologian-in-residence. I want the pastor to be the pastor-theologian-administrator who understands and experiences the faith, shepherds his or her people in nurturing care so that they both understand and experience, and aggressively shares that kind of call to others to come and share. Many will not buy. On the other hand, there are many waiting to know where the chameleonlike church does stand, and they will be responsive to forthrightness. We will gain some, not as many as *via* the McGavran-Schuller route, but those who do respond will know that it is for a distinctiveness unlike this world.

We can model the above. That is not the problem. The problem is the willingness to live in the creative tension that this model demands.

Creative Tension

After World War II, millions of people accepted the privilege afforded of withdrawing from the established church in Germany. For some it was simply a matter of avoiding the payment of church taxes. For others it was a matter of conscience because they had no personal religious commitment. But for many others it was a protest against a church that had blessed a culture and silenced its voice as a survival tactic, a church that had divorced salvation and liberation. The church whose growth this world needs is a church that struggles with salvation and emancipation, redemption and liberation. There are people outside the church who would come in if they were sure the church had this kind of integrity. Too often they have discerned that we have sold substance short.

The tension which this kind of ministry and this kind of church invites can be found in studying the ministry of a German Christian who refused to bless the culture of his time. His life and ministry might well be for us today a "paradigm" needed for a positive ministry of growth. It will be a ministry and a church characterized by certain ambivalences. I will list those ambivalences with a brief description.

Religious–Nonreligious

Dietrich Bonhoeffer was the most religious of humans; yet he was against religion. He it was who talked about "religionless Christianity" and followed Karl Barth's belief that "religion may be man's last stronghold against God." When I say that he was against religion, I mean that he was against the formal religious activities that always blessed the state and the religious establishment and failed to make any moral evaluation of positions taken. The church in Germany reached a compromise with Hitler. As long as it did not speak against Hitler, its existence and subsidy were allowed to continue. During those difficult days when millions were being killed, the church was concerned with an "in-house" kind of salvation, divorced from events in the real world. Bonhoeffer had a great appreciation for the church, but it was this "protected" church that he saw as a threat to the essence of the Christian way. The church must *be* and *do*—or else all of its religion is false.

Christ–Jesus

Bonhoeffer had such a positive Christology that his primary life direction could be gathered posthumously from his papers to which the title *Christ the Center* was given. Yet he often championed Jesus, man for others, in such a way that some question whether he had a Christology. Here is the person who could speak of Christ as the God for others, thus undergirding what he called the "religious interpretation" of the gospel. Yet he often preferred, in order to meet the social agnostics of any age, to emphasize the humanness of Jesus as the man for others. He could speak of incarnation but often as a humane concern interceding for others. He could speak of crucifixion as the love dimension of God, but he often meant an active suffering in order to shoulder the needs of others. He called this "commitment," the kind of commitment in which the image of an autocratic God and an autocratic pastor must die and the realization of a brotherly, committed God must live. He could speak of resurrection, but often he, in hope, was speaking of it as the long breath of patience in the daily struggle.

There was a higher theology of Christ; yet this was a theology that became an anthropology, the theology of a Christ incarnated and humiliated. The church thus shares the message and becomes the message about the glorification of God who seeks his honor in becoming man. The church and its ministry will thus walk not as a king but as a beggar among beggars. The God of the gospel will not be found in heaven but among people in real life, in the fellowship of the human.

Institutional–Secular

Dietrich Bonhoeffer was an institutional person; yet he often had to forsake the institution to live in the secular, noninstitutional world with "man come of age." Even when he insisted on life in the discipline of the institution, it was for the purpose of preparing to lead a life in a world of conflict. The church will share actively in the sufferings and struggles of the world even as Christ did. There are not two rooms in the world; Christianity is the center of reality. The reflective moves into the active; the spiritual goes into the natural; the holy moves into the secular; revelation moves into reality.

Universalist–Christian

Bonhoeffer had a sensitivity for all people everywhere and truly felt at times that the aetheist might be the most honest servant of God. He was thoroughly ecumenical in the fullest sense of the word. He faced seriously the question of being a member of the world church; yet he was a German and a member of the Lutheran church. It was he who was hesitant to take advantage of a captive audience and preach an Easter sermon, lest Ko-Korim, nephew of Molotov and an unbeliever, be misused as a captive, and yet who, when encouraged by Ko-Korim, preached the last sermon of his life and affirmed, "Good-bye, dear friends. This is the end—for me the beginning of life."

We have turned to Bonhoeffer in searching for a *positive* ministry of growth in order to indicate that *positive* growth is not only growth in numbers but also growth in substance—and this means a willingness to live in the ambivalence of creative tension. The Bonhoeffer emphasis serves as a corrective to much of that church growth material which suggests that the Christian life is primarily church-centered and must so order itself that maintaining the institution becomes its chief end. Bonhoeffer contributes balance. Even as the Bible is a divine-human book and Jesus is a divine-human person, so the church is a divine-human institution.

Getting Started

How does one get started in developing a positive ministry of growth that keeps in tension the need to grow and the call to faithfulness? If we approach the question from the perspective of a new pastor establishing oneself in a new place, the first thing one must do is to "get the lay of the land," i.e., establish a relationship with the church. Although the processes learned by experience elsewhere are transportable, it should be assumed that the programs are not transportable. Both quantitative and qualitative growth may be worthy goals, but one needs time for the church to sense ownership of those goals. Likewise, the specific methodology must be suited to this particular time and this particular place. Church growth materials, like denominational materials, are most helpful when they suggest principles and processes and place upon the local church the burden of developing specifics. The art of listening in order to sense "what is" and "where is" is a prerequisite. Listening demands patience, the long look, what Bonhoeffer called the "long breath." This gives an opportunity of becoming acquainted with the heritage and legacies from the past. It is wise to honor the past and to bless it without at the same time putting it into concrete. Except in those few instances here and there in which one runs into a predecessor who is insensitive to appropriate ethics, it is both helpful and honorable to recognize and pay homage to the contribution of one's predecessor. These people are our colleagues. Of course there are allegiances to former pastors. These need to be recognized. The particular pastor who has walked through a crisis situation with an individual or with a family will always be special. There is nothing wrong with that. If we honor that context of meaning and affirm it, that same individual or family usually gives us the opportunity of establishing similar relationships when the right moment develops. The styles and emphases of pastors are different. I have made a study of the pastors in the church where I serve, and it is interesting that across the years there has been an alternation between the aggressive-conflict-using types and the healing-fellowshipping types. Each era needs a different emphasis. What was right for one period may not be right for another. Every congregation must do its grief work when there is a severance of pastoral relationship. This takes time. Instead of shunning the past pastor, it may be wise to invite him or her back as vacation supply. People will appreciate that but usually at the same time discover that the different period and different time call for a different contribution. Through the invitation for the return, you have both gained a friend and made a supporter of your predecessor and, at the same time, "defanged" those whose emotions led them to believe that nothing could ever again be as great as what once was. Except for those sick people who can only live in the past, most people in the faith community will recognize the pull of the future if we ourselves are not so insecure as to send out false and defensive signals. During these "listening" periods of learning, analyzing, and affirming (usually about four years) we are establishing credibility ourselves by doing those things that have been called "paying the rent."

This is also the most intensive teaching phase of the pastoral relationship. Biblical rootage is surveyed. The Bible is our bread and butter. It is important to share in such a way as to come to an understanding on the nature of the biblical revelation. If I can detect flexibility and growth in this area, I know that my administrative task in initiating program and methodology is going to be much easier. Although intellectual perceptions are important during this period, it is the attitudinal stance with which I am most concerned. Emotional blockages are going to be found or shattered in the area of attitude rather than in some particular "doctrine" to be accepted or rejected. I would prefer the ultimate intellectual conclusions to grow out of experiential relationships. The biblical work is done through public worship, study occasions, and small groups. I often hear pastors speak of the intransient nature of women's societies. In every instance I have invited myself to do biblical work with these groups and have found them to be allies of support and change. Theological perceptions and conclusions are gradually being drawn through this biblical work. The theological perceptions enable one to explore the basic shepherding, fellowshipping, missional, worshiping, educative, and stewardship functions of ministry. Bible and theology fill these with content. The next step is most naturally to inquire for a vehicle, a methodology in order to facilitate the functions. In a word, these earlier years are an exploration together of the nature of the church.

The biblical and theological base aid in shaping program. As this phase of the work develops, the pastor's task involves administrative aspects, but one's role in the administrative is more facilitating than dominating. It is helpful if the pastor is viewed, not as a manager of the institution, but as a manager of the process. Facilitating management employs the "orchestra leader" aspects, facilitating each member (minister) of the parish to make his or her unique contribution. This also enhances a larger ownership of the goals and objectives. The method throughout is relational, and the style is more evolutionary than revolutionary. The art of listening never ceases. Committee meetings are not merely "administration." They are opportunities of ministry. Listening to contributions in committee sessions enables one to learn where people are most wounded. It is there that we pick up the person's story, and everyone has one. Knowing the story aids us in facilitating release not only from the hurt but also of more creative energies from the individual. Facilitating is a positive approach to administration in which one assumes the goodness of people. The congregation is viewed as the people of God and the members individually are fellow pilgrims. Patience is a virtue where voting on issues is not pressed until the climate is right. One is not seeking to get a "bill passed," but rather to grow a ministry. Delegation, assignment, and trust will be the order of the day.

Although the pastor may well assume that he or she is "the first among equals," he or she does not seek always to be the "up front" person. Time will be spent with lay leadership in planning, but the community will be healthier and happier if the execution of plans is in the hands of the membership. One of the negative aspects of multiple-staffed churches is the assumption that the staff persons are paid to do work that otherwise would have to be done by the laity. Over a period of years it is easy to forget that the ministers are all the members of the congregation and a misplaced expectancy arises. The pastor will, over a period of time, help to create another set of expectations and will seek to create both the process and the atmosphere for a larger involvement in ministry. When the process has been established, the pastor is wise who backs off and "risks" the process. Whatever the goal or the task, it will be assumed that all of the members have gifts. An effort is made to help in the discovery, recognition, and use of these gifts. Administration will be viewed as an opportunity to concretize some of the biblical and theological perspectives, and not simply as a time-consuming demand or problem. The method is the gentle method of persuasion and consent. The pastor in the process is not besieged as a fireman putting out fires, as a traffic cop, nor living in tension as a tightrope walker. The pastor is instead an orchestra leader who works with the community of faith, seeking to have a part in releasing the creative energies and efforts of all.

5

The Shape of
the Local Parish

The patient biblical and theological worker will uncover the six basic functions of ministry for any church of whatever polity. It is unfortunate that churches have been organized in patterns similar to the boards and mentalities of American corporations. Structures need to facilitate the functions of ministry. Deacons, stewards, elders, or whatever name leaders are called are needed as ministers rather than merely as board members who hear reports. We spend so much time "sitting" that we deceive ourselves into believing that we are engaged in ministry. It is hoped that every deacon, steward, or elder will be involved in one of the six functional areas of ministry to be described below. Over a period of several years in a church's life, this should become the prerequisite for election or appointment.

The transfer from the "board" mentality to the "ministry" mentality can be a very creative process. Tension in that process will be both inevitable and desirable for growth arises from creative tension. During the careful process of transfer, effort will be made to foster psychological *safety* in which the self-esteem of each person is reinforced by the absence of judgmental evaluations and attitudes. Psychological *freedom* will be fostered in which each person is encouraged to express ideas, feelings, and needs in socially appropriate and responsible ways. Some resistances will be experienced. Continuity is comfortable, and at times all of us fear the unfamiliar, are threatened by impotence in areas where we have held power, and have anxiety about the future use of power.[1] If the process is not rushed, if there is a sense of timing, and if the biblical, theological, and facilitating work has been done, the openness to new experience will also be there;

defensiveness and rigidity will be at a minimum; and the "let's try it" spirit will prevail. The one Spirit of God, nurtured by prayer and devotion, will contribute to the goal of individual growth and change, which, in turn, will make possible, both qualitatively and quantitatively, organizational growth and change. With a vision beyond institutional housekeeping, we will be conscious of witness and ministry and give intentionality to our spiritual growth, evangelism, and recruitment (numerical growth). Biblical roots will be prominent, and prayerful effort will be made to help the institution truly to reflect the body of Christ. Through the six functional shapes of ministry, we wish both to nurture and empower the members to translate the message of the gospel through the individual and corporate life-styles.

Six Basic Functions of Ministry

The Shepherding Ministry

Part of our ministry is to one another in a conserving and nurturing way. One lonely day during World War II when I was very disturbed and dejected at the harried pace of being a foot soldier, my unit suddenly broke through a clearing in the woods into a pastoral scene in a remote section of Germany. There in the valley in front of us was a shepherd tending sheep as if totally oblivious to a war-torn world or that we or anyone else were anywhere around. It was all so serene, so peaceful, and so therapeutic. I have remembered that scene many times across the years, for in the midst of the many prophetic tasks of the church and the business of tackling a secular world, there is always the shepherding function of the church. We are shepherds to one another, and we minister to the needs of all of the members. One of the earliest decisons of the early church was to become a fellowship of Jews and Gentiles, ministering to one another's needs, caring like shepherds for one another. It takes only a casual reading of the record of most churches to discover that an inordinate amount of time, effort, and money has been spent on ministering to the needs of the institution rather than in ministering to the needs of one another.

Recently I have been working through a huge, comprehensive volume on psychiatry, entitled *The Harvard Guide to Modern Psychiatry*.[2] I have been surprised to read section after section in which the psychiatrists are calling for a more personal touch on the part of psychiatrists, a personal listening, caring, and feeling for the patients. In one instance the book calls for *agape*, Christian love, as the only means for positive growth in health. Another part of the volume spells out the human need for inner support and security, not the support of material things or position, as the only way to alleviate anxiety so characteristic of our time. Yet the routine character of the American church is so often the opposite and is becoming increasingly so with the so-called "electronic church," which is gathering millions of dollars each year and is more intent on building empires for TV religious figures than in facilitating the quality of Christian personal life as we become more sensitive, like shepherds, in ministering to the needs, the bruises and the wounds, and the lostness of one another.

The Old Testament has many images of shepherds as the symbol of ministry. Jesus claimed the same for himself: "I am the good shepherd . . ." (John 10:11). That was the way the early Christians in the days of their trial and persecution loved to depict him, for on the walls of the catacombs where they often had to hide to worship, there are etched scenes of Jesus as the Good Shepherd with his sheep standing around him and earnestly gazing into his face.

A shepherding ministry is built on the model of the shepherd who not only gathers, feeds, and watches the flock, but also runs some risk for it. Every evidence is that we will not truly be the continuing incarnation until we, too, have the faith that gives us the freedom to risk loving and helping one another. If we within the church have never risked our lives for one another, our humanity has been tragically diminished. Perhaps our Lord does not literally bid us come and die, but he does call us to such a quality of relationships—the quality of shepherding care for one another—that should death come, it would be all right. One of the passages which means more to me than any other in pointing to the shepherding function of the church is 2 Corinthians 1:3-4—"Blessed be the God and Father of our Lord Jesus Christ, the Father of mercies and God of all comfort, who comforts us in all our affliction, so that we may be able to comfort those who are in any affliction, with the comfort with which we ourselves are comforted by God." How could anything be clearer? We have the call of Christ to extend his loving comfort as the shepherd people. "Feed my lambs and tend my sheep" was a resurrection instruction of Jesus. In that instruction lies the biblical understanding of shepherding and caring: helping to nurture others along the way and *tending,* i.e., giving enough attention to provide structure for their lives.

Baptism is the Christian's ordination to shepherding. The call to be a shepherd is a call to help create a supportive environment. It is participation in healing through making oneself available by a smile of kindness or a quality of relationship that aids in overcoming impairment and brokenness by warming someone else on the road to wholeness. It is sustaining, helping a person endure or transcend a circumstance where restoration or recuperation is improbable. It is guiding, helping people to make confident choices between alternative courses of thought and action. It is reconciling, building bridges between broken relationships. Fundamental to the Christian journey is the knowledge that we do not travel alone, that we need someone to help us in a spiritual companionship. Although in no way denigrating the need for professionals in the deepest traumas of life, psychiatry reminds us that 90 percent of the real help people receive comes from their friends and not through highly trained and paid professionals. The church is a family in which multiple fathers, mothers, brothers, and sisters "put heart" into one another. Where this kind of community is achieved and made known, others will be attracted to it, for the need is well established.

The creation of the climate may take some time, but once the climate is established, it is rather simple to divide the membership into shepherding groups. Each shepherding group will have a deacon or other person who makes it his or her responsibility regularly to check with each name or family under his or her care to keep open the communication channel. From time to time—monthly, quarterly, semiannually as the situation warrants—the shepherding group might meet in a home, at a restaurant, on a picnic, or at some recreational or social engagement for the purpose of maintaining a "sense of family." The shepherd leader will regularly be in telephone contact with his or her cadre of people. Straying or wounded people are soon discovered and remedial care given.

Other categories of service within the shepherding ministry are hospital and nursing home calling. Workshops and congregational events of nurture and care are made available through the shepherding ministry. Home Communion and tape services for nonattenders are part of the shepherding ministry. The elderly are systematically and routinely supported. The shepherding ministry is involved in integrating functions like the discovery and use of human resources, sponsorship for new members, attendance, and membership classes. Shepherding seeks to provide those "entry" points into the life of the congregation. It may be great to have a tremendous sense of fellowship and "comradarie," but if there are no entry points for newcomers who need to be nurtured and supported, it appears that the church is a closed corporation. Whether a church is that way, in fact, or is only perceived that way, the end result is the same—dropouts.

The Fellowshipping Ministry

Closely related to shepherding is fellowship. The life of the early church was characterized by fellowship: "And they devoted themselves to the apostles' teaching and fellowship, to the breaking of bread and the prayers" (Acts 2:42). The purpose of their ministry was to share fellowship: "that which we have seen and heard we proclaim also to you, so that you may have fellowship with us; and our fellowship is with the Father and with his Son Jesus Christ" (1 John 1:3). Because the life of eternity is to abide in love, it can only be lived in community. Thus, fellowship is both the goal and the source of proclaiming the Christian message. Human nature is made for fellowship, but the fellowship of people with God and with one another through Christ is the richest fellowship. Likewise, it alone fulfills the purpose of life, "that you may be children of your Father who is in heaven" (Matthew 5:45).

Religion is not just "individual" in nature. For that reason it is not satisfactory merely to have religion by proxy by radio or by television. Merely individual religion is a contradiction in terms. Our spiritual life is inevitably mutual. Mysticism, a kind of just being gathered up into God by oneself, at times has a place in the Christian life, but one of the most mystical of all Christians, the author of the epistle of First John, does not err when he habitually uses the plural "we," which with "us" and "our" appears some twelve times in his first ten verses. The divine-human fellowship of believers with one another in Christ constitutes the life of the church and exposes by contrast the cheap forms of so-called fellowship in which some groups specialize.

The true nature of the church's fellowship is portrayed in Jesus' metaphor of the vine and the branches (John 15) and in Paul's metaphor of the body (Romans 12; 1 Corinthians 12). Rooted in Christ, we are intertwined like grapevines in self-sacrificing love and given to mutual service, prayer, labor, and helpfulness. Today when people meet or do business in someone's office, or as they leave the church building, we shake hands. Shaking hands was early used as an expression of the full fellowship established by common faith in Christ. As Paul expressed it in his Galatian letter, "When they perceived the grace that was given to me, James and Cephas and John. . . . [they] gave to me and Barnabas the right hand of fellowship . . ." (Galatians 2:9). Shaking hands is not just "something we do." It grows out of public acknowledgment that we share a life and faith together, commonly rooted in Christ. Shaking hands is affirming something about Christ and about community. This touching of the hands is a reminder that there is an interdependence that binds us closely together in mutual life, support, and encouragement.

Koinonia (fellowship) is the word found so frequently within the Greek community. It means to "share with someone in something." It means to give someone a share in something; it is a partnership. Participating in the fellowship of the church is sharing in the humility and glory and even in the suffering of Christ. The common sharing there leads us to share in one another's humility, glory, and suffering. What individually are weaknesses become strengths as we, like weak sticks, are bound together in a strong bundle (Ezekiel 37:15-23). Fellowship is not a kind of "religious civic club" where as a happy crowd we eat lunch together, say superficial things to each other, and go our way until next week's luncheon. Fellowship is somehow connected with "steadfastness in the apostles' teaching." The earliest Christians had no creed, but they did have an experience. The sharing of the meaning of that experience constituted the teaching. The teaching was made up of the personal contributions, the "sharings," of those present. They told what it meant that they had been with Jesus, and this became the content of the teaching that was shared. Deposits and

withdrawals from that common sharing created a common life and perspective, a koinonia.

Likewise, those early Christians knew they could not meet life in their
own strength, and so they went in to God before they went out into the
world. Fellowship is rooted in prayer. We get to know someone and feel
closer to someone when we spend time in prayer together. Separate coals
from one another, and they do not burn well. Put them together and there
is a briskness of fire. Children of the Christian family take heart through
the fellowship of prayer.

Fellowship is likewise nurtured by the breaking of bread. "And they
devoted themselves to . . . fellowship, to the breaking of bread. . . ." In
the beginning every common meal was hallowed by a remembrance of
Jesus. To break bread together is to "remember Jesus." Across the years
the Lord's Supper has changed until now it is a separate entity by itself.
But it should concern us and challenge us that those first believers hallowed
common things and common food by partaking of it with the memory of
His great sacrifice in mind. When the church eats together in its many
meals and suppers, let it be consciously aware that even the poorest fare,
the coarsest bread on the humblest table, may become a memorial of our
dear Lord and bring back ever sweeter fellowship. And when we eat at
home with our families, let us remember that the common meals of the day
bind the sacred and the secular together. And whenever there are those
special times when we gather for the Communion, or Eucharist, let us be
mindful that those who partake of the Supper are Christ's companions. You
may even desire to sit closer to your neighbor, for there is a fellowship
with the Lord and a fellowship among the participants. Fellowship arises
from a common union with him, even as Christ is represented by one loaf.
Fellowship is an interdependence through a great fellowshipping network
nurtured by common roots in Christ.

This of necessity is a function of ministry. Although fellowship cannot
be created, it can be facilitated and nurtured. The fellowshipping ministry,
therefore, seeks to find ways of providing an ongoing experience of deeply
meaningful community through corporate and primary group relationships.
Here, again, the ministry of the laity is essential. Routine things take on
a larger dimension as the fellowshipping context is provided. Activities that
once were mechanical in nature now assume a larger dimension. Food
service, receptions, and socials, picnics, and coffee hours are part of the
fellowship life. The church's life of prayer is a vital part of this group's
ministry. The fellowshipping ministry will provide opportunities through
many kinds of small groups—care groups, prayer groups, worship groups,
growth groups—and through seasonal groups, such as during Advent and
Lenten periods. Home and Sunday evening fellowships of various kinds
will come into the picture.

The Worshiping Ministry

It is my firm conviction that more opportunity for stimulation to growth and change lies within the worship area than in any other phase of the church's life. Here, again, the entire membership can have a part in this ministry, which is both for themselves and for the nonmembership.

The people of God will come back again and again to the experiential source of an inner fire with a deep sensitivity to the sacred. With the importance of small groups and all other activities of church life undisputed, worship and adoration still form the nerve center. It is here that we find an illuminating and empowering perspective on ourselves and on our neighbors. It is here that the sensitivity to the sacred is kept alive. It is in the worship of God that we find out who we are. Here we discover ourselves to be persons of worth, loved by God. Here we find the peace that the world about us cannot take away because the world did not give it to us. It is likewise in the adoration of God that we discover who our neighbor is. Here it is that we change gears and loosen our grip on resentment and hostility and recognize our brothers and sisters as also ones for whom Christ died. Most of all, it is in this sensitivity to the sacred that we come to know who God is. It is *this* adoration that gives us the right attitude toward ourselves and others. It is through worship that the gears of our lives are changed.

Worship is declaring worth to someone. "Worthy is the Lamb that was slain," and the tide continues to swell in the book of Revelation: "Blessing and honor and glory and power to him who sits upon the throne and to the Lamb forever and ever." Worship is response to God. The first act of worship is an act of reverence and awe, an attempt to show veneration and express thankfulness. In worship we are participants in an activity and not spectators in a performance. The worshiper is part of the act, not an observer, not the prayed for but the pray-*er*. Involvement is essential for one's sense of the holy and encounter with Christ. Worship is not a religious variety show to entertain but an expression of appreciation and love for God. Worship is a time for offering ourselves to God. The offering of gifts is a personal symbol of thanksgiving, dedication, and sacrifice. It represents self-giving. It is my conviction that every person who worships, including the children, should place an offering upon the altar of God. Worship celebrates both the visions by which life is transformed and the values that govern life.

We have discussed elsewhere the place of preaching in the life of worship. In all of worship, including the sermon, the laity has both an opportunity and a responsibility. From time to time various groups might come together with the preaching minister and read together the Scripture that is to be the sermon text or context a few weeks later. Members of the group present are asked what the passage said, what it means, and how it relates to us;

they are asked to specify what unanswered questions it raises. That material is incorporated into the sermon. There is never better listening response than on that occasion when *that* sermon is delivered, for all who participate wish to know whether it comes out as *their* sermon. Follow-up conversation extends the value of the experience.

The other end of that, of course, is the sermon listening group of various kinds. The most helpful kind I have found is a group of some six to eight people gathering around a tape recorder right after the sermon. Each week a member of the group is responsible for involving five additional people the following week so that over a period of time a cross section of the congregation is involved. The people sit together and speak to questions such as: "What do you think the minister said this morning? What do you think he meant by what he said? How well did she say it? Do you agree or disagree with what he said? What do you think she should have said?" At some time during the week, the pastor listens to the responses and where there are matters of significance telephones the participants and engages in further conversation. Preaching thus becomes a congregational task and stays alive.

These occasions underscore the basic conviction that worship is a corporate act and that preaching is a community responsibility, that over a period of years it is the community that preaches. The preacher is the agent of the dialogue, but the sermon can be a community experience. Through such processes both proclamation *(kerygma)* and teaching *(didache)* are interwoven. Preaching becomes an instrument of worship that speaks both to the non-Christian world and to the Christians.

Of course the pastor provides a guiding hand in worship, but the service of worship, the opportunities of worship, the preparation of worship and the leadership of worship are not his or her design alone. Lay people have long been involved in arrangements for certain phases of worship life—ushers, flowers, assistance with baptism and Communion and other operational functions. But the laity are equally well equipped both to articulate and respond to the deeper questions of worship: Whom do we worship? How can we best symbolize and realize our human relation to God through worship? Is it valid to seek to fulfill human needs in worship, and what are those needs? How are the other functions of church symbolized and expressed in worship? The worshiping ministry is involved in finding the best ways and means of enabling people to worship God and to celebrate and dramatize the meaning of the church's life together. The lay leadership will give itself to development and training of worship-life and the provision of alternative worship opportunities. Special periods of worship, such as during Advent and Lent, will be under their direction. Constant education and worship promotion will be in the care of those who function in the worshiping ministry. Music and drama as alternative forms of worship will be explored.

Worship is concerned with an experience of God, and this is too serious a matter to be deposited in the hands of one or two professionals.

Thirsting for God and a restlessness for God are deep within the human struggle. Relatedness to God is the one needful thing and is like relinquishing everything in order to have the pearl of great price (Matthew 13:46) or the treasure hidden in the field (Matthew 13:44). The pastor will certainly be a primary resource person in staffing the worship cadre, but that cadre should be sufficiently representative of the myriads of people who are engaged in the restless struggle and hunger. This will afford the best opportunity for attracting an enlarged number to the answer to the quest.

The Missional Ministry

People engaged in the function of missional ministry have the responsibility of sensitizing the entire body of Christ. It is in this area that church growth and evangelization are constantly scrutinized.

When I was a lad growing up, in my home Sunday school there was nothing more exciting to me than to hear the exciting stories of missionary faith. I still get excited when I hear the faithful and daring stories of a Stanley and Livingston opening up the missionary frontiers of Africa or of a Dr. Albert Schweitzer in the medical missions of Lambarene. It is likewise stirring to hear of shoe cobbler William Carey, the Baptist who almost single-handedly in 1792 founded the modern missionary movement, defying his fellow British Baptists who said, "If God wants to save the Indians, he will do it on his own," and who responded, "Expect great things from God; receive great things from God; lengthen your chords and strengthen your stakes," and alone set out for India. My soul still stirs to the sacrificing commitment of a Dr. Marian Boehr from the church that I serve, a woman who carries on the great missionary tradition of healing and saving in an ill-equipped hospital that serves thousands in India today.

And yet with all that, across the years I have come to see the limitations. Missions was something you enabled someone else to do by sending your money. The stories were exciting, and the urgency of continuing that missionary pace continues. But now I know from the New Testament that missions is not just sending; it is going. The focus can no longer be placed on "they" and "them" as though mission and ministering to the world were reserved alone for some special group.

All of us are called to be involved in mission. The church has a mission. The individual Christian has a mission. "Missions" in terms of sending someone is but a small part of "mission." To be called to Christ is to be called to "go." The Great Commission was not given to a selected group. It is Christ's challenge to be incorporated into the life of every single believer. That mission begins with the concerns sponsored by the worshiping ministry. I can never forget that classic experience in Isaiah: ". . . I saw the Lord . . . high and lifted up. . . . And I said: 'Woe is me! For I am [sinful]. '. . . And [he said], '. . . who will go for us?' . . ." (Isaiah 6:1, 5, 8). When God reveals himself to a person, this is the most natural response to follow. An overwhelming realization of God's eternal holiness and a distressing sense of personal unworthiness are part of one's experience. Moses took off his shoes; Elijah covered his face; Isaiah fell apart on the inside and cried out in confession; Peter dropped to his knees. But it would be well to remember that an encounter with God, a true spiritual experience, is seldom an end in itself. God uses it to inspire and call participants to service. Isaiah's vision of God gave him his message, a mission, and a service to be filled.

And that is what mission is: it is service. Nowhere is that more beautifully seen than in that setting from the upper room, recorded only in John's Gospel as a legacy for us. Jesus gathered his disciples around himself, and they experienced the intense revelation of his loving presence as he knelt down with a foot basin of water, washed, and towel-dried the dirty, travel-soiled feet of each disciple and shared those beautiful words, "I have given you an example, that you should wash one another's feet. A new commandment I give to you, that you love one another; even as I have loved you. As the Father has loved me, so have I loved you; abide in my love" (see John 13:12-14, 34; 15:9). Love and service, another word for mission, go hand in hand. Experience and personal opportunity for ministry are part of the same setting. There is some kind of personal challenge to ministry in every experience with God.

That service and that ministry are to Christians. As the church we have a ministry to one another. And as a Christian it is quite legitimate to receive ministry, to receive comfort and nurture. Shepherding and fellowshipping represent some of those things that the church does for itself. The church is the community of acceptance, and one has the right to expect the loving care and support of other Christians. Often one has no place else to go for support. It is to be regretted that often Christians hide their wounds, for it denies Christian brothers and sisters the privilege of service and ministry to one another.

Ministering to the self is like feeding the body. The kitchen is a prominent feature in nearly every home. We spend a lot of time there and gain family fellowship there along with the physical nurture. Caring for the physical necessities of life is part of the expected good stewardship to ourselves, and we are poor stewards if we neglect it. The needs of the world outside the church are so large and Christ's mandate to minister to all of the world is so clear that we must constantly hear that call. But to do so is not to minimize the validity of the church ministering to itself, helping other Christians to experience the balm of Gilead and knowing that it is all right to be folded in the arms of Jesus, to find him as a resting place and a needed port in our time of storm. The fondest times of my life are those times when life was sagging and the church ministered to me.

The tragedy is when we become so self-centered as to forget that the mission to the inside is for the purpose of giving us that encouraging wholeness that enables us to engage in the ministry to the outside. Furthermore, our own needs often are best ministered to as we aid in building bridges to others.

The church must discover again that the ministry to the outside is primarily a lay ministry. It is now clear that if the huge ministry demanded by our kind of world is to be actuated, it must be a lay movement. The deprivation of the laity in mission and the exaltation of the clergy are offenses against the Body of Christ, for in the Body all are equally valued, though their functions differ. The membership of the churches constitutes an untapped resource of ministry. Clergy can aid in cultivating the harvest, but it is the lay witness that will win the world to Christ and the church. Clergy must aid in consciousness raising to the privilege and responsibility, but it is everyone's privilege to say a few words each week concerning his or her faith in Christ. In most cases even a sentence or two will set the tone. Even church growth would not be such a complicated matter if the average Christian determined to invite and bring one person to his or her church every two weeks.

The waiting world expects, even hopes, that we will bear our witness. People do not believe we mean business. We often do not have the sense of mission that is found in the pseudo-religions. Do we really mean to confront the world with the figure of Christ, or do we simply mean to get as much comfort as we can out of our religion and forget this mission to the outside? Effective ministry is through the lay Christians of the world and not through the glamour of the ''big time'' production.

The missional ministry is at the heart of the church's life. Those familiar functions are lodged there. National mission (home) and international mission (foreign) come under its care. Missionary education, the support of institutions, and correspondence with missionaries are all within its concern. But the neglected areas are community outreach, Christian social concern, and evangelism. I fail to understand the ''why'' of our concern for the people whom we cannot know in a distant place and our complacent lack of concern about the responsibility and opportunity of ministry with those people whom we meet every day.

The Educating Ministry

Perhaps we have not been as supportive and serious in our educating ministry as is needed. Perhaps we have failed to connect the missional and educating phases of ministry. Perhaps we have not rightly related the legacy of our heritage to empowerment for Christian ministry.

Jesus received his strength for ministry, at least in part, from his heritage from the past. When he was sorely tempted at the beginning of his ministry, he reached back into his stored biblical memory and three times from the Book of Deuteronomy found nourishing strength for his present task. When he was challenged with persecution in Galilee and caught in a soul struggle as to whether and how he would handle the future, he drew aside to a mountain place that we have come to call the Mount of Transfiguration, and he found his strength again in the searching of the Law and the Prophets represented by Moses and Elijah. Today's ministry always needs yesterday's heritage, and such is the concern of the educating ministry. The biblical records remind us of the importance of remembering what God has done in the past because strength and hope come from knowing that what God has done once, God may well do again.

The teaching of Jesus began with the Law and the Prophets; he affirmed them and added modifications and additions peculiarly related to his own person. Early Christians became disciples of this process. In the early church the name for a Christian was "disciple," meaning student or learner. Education for us is thus a combination of learning from yesterday and from today so that yesterday's roots produce a new growth, a new flowering. The Christian is not passive. Jesus was not interested in finding people who, for years to come, would do nothing more than sit and listen to him and perhaps support him financially in his mission. He was interested in making disciples who would be committed to share with him, in some measure, in his mission, a sharing that would be possible only if they were open to unending learning and growth.

It was and is not sufficient for a person to "make a profession of faith" and then merely become a good-living, loyal member of a Christian community. There was and is a world waiting to be conquered and transformed by faith. Therefore, what Jesus called into being was not an impressive new religious organization with the one purpose of maintaining the moral and spiritual life of the community at a respectable level but an *avant-garde* force of disciples who would themselves grow and invade the world with a sharing of what they themselves had experienced.

In 1980 we celebrated the two hundredth anniversary of the Sunday school movement, which was founded in 1780 by Robert Raikes. And because the Sunday school primarily began with children, we have somehow got the idea that learning is primarily a childen's event. But discipleship is a lifelong process. A medical doctor who has ceased to be a student of medicine is not likely to serve his or her patients well. He or she not only fails to learn of later developments in the treatment of diseases, but also in ceasing to be a student, he or she adopts a mental attitude that is injurious to his or her work. Neither are Christians to remain at a childhood level. Unfortunately, statistics show that a very small percentage of adult members of a church take part in any study or discipleship program or give any time to the study of their faith in private. Often even the church leadership is not so involved. When the leadership of a church is not involved in Bible study, not involved in regular corporate and private prayer, and is not involved in the educational life of the church, the spiritual substance diminishes.

When Jesus was facing the painful decision about the nature of his ministry and the suffering of the cross, he brought the past into the present. He sat down and learned from Moses and Elijah. Luke says that they spoke of "his departure," which he was to accomplish at Jerusalem. The word is *exodus*. They were discussing the great exodus experience as God's great salvation event and how it was central in God's creation of a people. Jesus, if faithful to his call, could be another *exodus,* a central event in God's reconciling call and creation of a people unto himself. The past and the present were brought into focus. People in our time often do not know Jesus and his significance for life because they do not know Moses and Elijah. As the disciples gathered with Jesus, it was in their confrontation with the revelation of God as they found it in the Law and the Prophets that they were prepared for the experience of glory in Jesus.

The educational ministry directs us to the source of our heritage as that heritage is recorded in the Scripture and through tradition. It is needful for us to go back to the history of our tradition, even as Jesus went back to the history of his tradition in Moses and Elijah. We cannot be the church and fail to recognize that we have a heritage, a biblical history. It is disturbing that many do not know what that heritage is. There are many for whom the Bible is a superstitious talisman, waved like a sword but not known in the heart. There are others who make no reference to the Bible at all, and, indeed, one suspects that the work of some Protestant congregations is done with no reference to the Bible at all.

Education enables us to know the heritage and to reflect upon that heritage. Jesus did not go up into the mountain to be transfigured. He went up to pray and through prayer the heritage came better into view. When we reflect upon the past, we often embody its strengths. Likewise, when Jesus prayed, reflecting and meditating on the gifts from the lawgivers and prophets, he received clues and guidance for his destiny in the future.

The educational ministry reminds us that one never looks to the heritage to become stuck or glued in a backward look, but in order to carry forward a valid continuation of what was done. Jesus was in no sense repeating the work of Moses and Elijah. He was carrying it forward to a greater completion. The discipleship of which education is a part has its roots in yesterday, but the thrust is in tomorrow. Ours is a living heritage.

A church of disciples who know they are disciples will be a school of Christ in which both the gospel and the world to which it is addressed will be studied, but always in preparation for the invasion of the world with the gospel of reconciliation. A church that does not lead into mission is sterile, but mission without thorough education in our biblical heritage in preparation for it invites frustration. It is not enough to have rusty shields and rusty swords. If we are not engaged in the educational ministry, we are like soldiers in the midst of battle but without weapons.

Of course, the educating ministry involves the traditional church school. Far more, however, it is involved in a plethora of discipling opportunities that are both in-house and out-of-house. Home experiences are part of that ministry. Task forces in this ministry service scholarships, educational institutions, and other functions that may or may not be vitally related to discipleship. Programs of education for the geographical community in which the church building is located may also be involved. Sometimes linkage with other institutions in the area to provide opportunities and seminars in the areas of lower and higher education may be the best way to cultivate recruitment possibilities at a later date.

The Stewardship Ministry

The growth of the church, qualitatively and quantitatively, is ultimately related to faithfulness in stewardship, using stewardship as a very broad term.

Jesus began his ministry in Galilee. When persecution set in there, he traveled to Jerusalem for an open challenge to the sin and irreligion of his time. On the way south there was an incident at the border of the Samaritan territory, which more than any other story in all the Gospels spells out human ingratitude (Luke 17:11-19). Just as Jesus was about to skirt the territory, he met a band of ten lepers, nine Jews and one Samaritan. Common misery and need drove them together in spite of their "unlikeness." Jesus cured the lepers and sent them to report to the priest. There were ten of them and only one of them, the Samaritan, returned to give thanks. The primary thrust of the narrative is not the ability of Jesus to cure lepers but the attitude of the person cured. And in that attitude of thanksgiving was found a new blessing: "Rise and go your way, your faith has made you well."

The stewardship work of the church will arise from the positive spirit of appreciation. Our work is not a mandate; it is a response. Wholeness is a matter of the spirit, a matter of the inner life, and that kind of blessing is grounded in the appreciative life. Right belief in a church is important, but there are many who believe who are not ready to praise. All nine of the lepers had some kind of belief, but only one of them came back to praise. Praise is the test of true belief. Few afflictions of the spirit can match ingratitude, the dread habit of taking things for granted in the absence of the grateful heart.

The penalty of ingratitude is the closing of the door against the deeper blessings of life. Jesus does not withdraw his gifts because they are not appreciated. The nine lepers had been healed and remained healed. But Jesus could not lift them into the circle of a larger relationship because, through thoughtlessness, they were not available to his larger touch. And when we do not position ourselves to receive more of Christ's touch, we lose the joy of that which we have.

In our churches we normally approach stewardship in terms of the use of the material things that we manage in behalf of God. That certainly is a large part of stewardship and is perhaps the test of whether we are worthy stewards. Prudent management is expected of us. One of the more difficult parables (Luke 16:1-13) is of a manager who saved his own neck by collecting reduced debts from his master's debtors. On the surface it may appear that the man was complimented for his roguery and rascality. Further exploration finds the key in the comment of Jesus ". . . the children of this world are wiser than the children of light" (see verse 8). Slovenly methods and disinterest of spirit are not acceptable in the Lord's work. Resourceful and courageous action are joined to the positive spirit of appreciation as the church does its work. Great things would happen if appreciative people brought to the work of the church and kingdom even half of the resolution, resourcefulness, and determination that are routinely expected in the secular world.

Too frequently in the church we look upon our "problems" rather than our "opportunities." Creative strategizing calls for us to use resources in new ways as we approach the opportunities. If the church adopts the mentality of self-pity because of all of those problems out there, it is likely to hoard its resources rather than invest them. "Feeling sorry" is one of the most disintegrating forces that can play upon either an individual or an institution. We also make less than prudent response in the church through a tendency to feel that we are so small in terms of the task to be done. This again results from a failure of thankful response to the God of the cosmos. The most tremendous forces in the world for good are not huge and planetary. Prudent Christian action plus God can make an eternity of difference.

Stewardship is responding to God with who we are and what we have where we are. It is the cultivation of the positive, thankful spirit that dares to make investments of what already is God's. The Christian faith is not lived in the spirit of selfishness, seeking to get by with as little as possible. Rather, it is lived with the spirit of thankfulness, seeking to do as much as possible for God. In turn, the cost of being a disciple of Jesus is all that one is and has. It is not enough to savor the life nor taste it; it is not a part-time effort. Christian discipleship costs everything that one is and everything that one has, and it needs to be presented that way.

There is nothing about the Christian life that denies the joy in the use of material things. The material world is the work of God, and God called his work good. The material world is a sacrament of the gift of God for human enjoyment, and the Christian life never minimizes the physical necessities of existence. It was Jesus who taught us to pray, "Give us this day our daily bread." But the church, the continuing incarnation, must know that until the cry for bread—and that includes the cry for a decent home and a wholesome environment and a just social order—is answered, there can be no rest for the church and Christ and for any who call him Lord. Providing for all of these cries, too, is stewardship.

The church does not talk about money as filthy. The test is its use or abuse. Money is an important ingredient of good food and healthy homes, of education and recreation, of churches and hospitals and neighborhood centers, and missions across the globe. How great that God has made us stewards! Discipleship costs in the materialism that we surrender, but how wonderful to be a part of an operating theater in India, the Philippines, or South America; how wonderful to see bodies mended, death successfully resisted, spirits being lifted, lives being redeemed, a person rescued from waywardness on the streets in the city—because the church is there! Thanks be to God that we may express appreciation to him through investments in the well-being of humankind everywhere.

It is this spirit that motivates the stewardship ministry. It is this spirit that creates a vision of ministry. It is within that vision that there will be neither timidity nor hesitancy in exploring the church's need for financial resources or in the same exploration of the need of Christians to express their commitment both tangibly and symbolically with their resources. This ministry has the function of making proper use of existing resources as an example of stewardship, planning for future needs and establishing programs of additional income and educating the congregation on the stewardship of funds and resources. Many tasks are involved, such as planning in personal and family stewardship, physical plant and facilities management, the legal aspects of church business, financial management, stewardship awareness through seminars and other educational media, churchwide training and promotion, financial planning relative to estates, wills and trusts, budget making and financial control, fund raising, propery management, etc. Where "trustees" are desired or required, they will be "servants of thanksgiving" and "facilitators of ministry" rather than mere property managers. If that which we manage and to which we have access does not facilitate ministry, then its very availability is a curse rather than a blessing.

Pastoral Support

Each of the areas of ministry is chaired by a lay person. The goal is the involvement of laity in every aspect of the church's ministry. The pattern is suitable for a very small or a very large congregation. The pastor's and/or staff's responsibility is to provide motivation and the appropriate resources—biblical, theological, or otherwise—for the ministering sections. Each of the functional areas of ministry will devise as many committees and/or short-range task forces as are needed for accomplishing its work. An advisory/executive group will be composed of the pastor/staff, the chairpersons of each area of ministry, and the elected officers of the church. Periodically, all areas of ministry will meet in a combined session for the purposes of business, nurture, and education. These general sessions will provide the opportunity for setting the primary direction that all areas of ministry are pursuing. At least once a quarter the combined meeting will be dedicated solely to inspiration and nurture. Resource persons outside of the congregation and its staff will be valuable. The advisory/executive group provides continuity with the areas of ministry. The particular areas of ministry will meet on a regular basis, at least once a month, and the committees and subsections will meet as often as helpful.

Church growth and other goals will be kept before the church and before the areas of ministry by the pastor and staff. If such goals are adopted by the entire church and each area of ministry works on the common goal from its particular assignment of responsibility, success is more easily within grasp.

The Larger Community

Every congregation finds motivation through involvement with a larger judicatory or denominational unit that is working on the same premises, with the same perspective, and with similar goals. Congregations are not, however, so situated geographically that kindred units are always near. Although contrary to the counsel of church growth specialists, it is of the utmost urgency to reach out to neighboring congregations of whatever denomination in order to develop mission-oriented units and to develop a sense of the "presence" of the church in that particular community. This is especially needful in urban society. Units of four to six congregations each can develop a powerful thrust and exhibit sufficient strength so that through its activities, the geographical community perceives an awareness that the "church" is here.

A most challenging illustration is the ministry of the "Focus" churches in Albany, New York. In the early 1970s four downtown congregations met in a retreat setting to explore common concerns of ministry. Subsequently a coordinating committee was constituted by staff and lay representatives of each of the four congregations. Across the years there have been many common ventures of ministry and combined education and worship. In the initial period, there was that cautious suspicion as to what the "other" group had to gain or what "our group" had to give up. I was one of the organizing pastors, and I well remember the low level of our trust toward one another. The motivation was sincere, however, and the four congregations created a budget pool so that behavioral specialists could come and work with the pastors in a retreat setting so as to help build the bridge of trust. Since that time there have been shared staff, shared budget, shared outreach, and planning in almost any area one can imagine.

The larger community is far more aware of the presence of the church than it might have been had each congregation insisted on isolation and separateness. Areas of commonality have elicited a loyalty to the whole (called Focus) and an appreciation for the peculiar ministries that each congregation can best do in its own style and for its own purposes. Biblical and theological appreciation have increased since the common life together has challenged presuppositions. An American Baptist, a United Methodist, and two United Presbyterian churches constitute Focus. The denominational loyalties and doctrinal tenets are more enlightened and, where challenged, more firmly held because each church found it necessary to understand its tenets in order to know what it had to contribute to the larger entity. None of the congregations has in any sense been diminished by the cooperation in common ministry. The strength of the whole has contributed to the strength of the individual units.

The growth of the church in difficult urban society is likely to be through some pattern as that of the Focus churches. The star of individual churches may rise and fall from time to time, but this kind of endeavor makes known the presence of the church in the larger community at all times. Where individual units have so organized themselves for cooperative endeavor, an administrator (bishop, supervising pastor) might be elected on a rotating basis so that leadership continuity and coordination might be given. The pattern might well give strength to those struggling congregations who need the encouragement to savor life. Far more, it provides an avenue for strong congregations to share strengths, become stronger, and widen the influence of ministry. These cooperative units of congregations can form linkages with other units of congregations within the city or environs. This "wholeness" of the church strengthens the ministry of Christ throughout the larger community. Influenced by the church, people recognize their need for the church and seek to become part of the Body of Christ through whichever unit or local congregation is most compatible to them.

A Postscript

Growth in the contemporary church will not come by any one pattern. The technical movement symbolized by the School of World Mission and Institute of Church Growth has much to offer. I have tried to be fair in presenting its strengths. I have likewise tried to point out some very grave dangers within its premises. There was a day when I thought black was black and white was white. I no longer recognize such absolutes. It is because McGavran's movement insists on such absolutes that I am disturbed. It is because much of the church has no absolutes at all in terms of responsibility for growth that I am pained. Most of life has some hybrid nature about it. It is with deliberateness that I would borrow from McGavran and from the ecumenical movement. Each has strengths to contribute. The end result will be rather eclectic, as ministry is tailor-made for each particular situation.

Whatever patterns are developed must be evaluated by a theological understanding of the nature of the church. Anything that excludes one group of people in favor of another must be questioned. Techniques cannot be used simply because "they work." Our task is not to build a successful institution. It is to be the church. Faithfulness at being the church may at times repel rather than attract numbers. Therefore, to be driven by a mandate that everything must get "bigger and better" all the time is a false mandate. Numerical success may in some instances be graphic testimony that the church has failed to be the church. Sociological data and commercial marketing techniques must not be elevated beyond the evaluation of biblical and theological faithfulness.

One of the things that concerns me about the church growth movement is its sense of dogmatism. Throughout its literature there is a biblical and theological stance that seems to suggest that if you are not of "our kind," you are not faithful and may be less than Christian. Such arrogance is repulsive. I have learned much from the church growth movement. I wish there were evidence of an openness that might suggest that learning is a two-way process.

I do believe that church growth provides a much needed challenge and stimulus to the church in general. Simply to believe in what you are doing is not enough, but it does help. Main-line churches do seem often so terribly tired and despairing with a defeatest mentality. It is helpful to be reminded that God is still at work and that he wishes to do much of his work through us. It is helpful, too, to be called away from that pseudo-tolerance where "anything goes." We do have a "precious treasure," and the grace of God is that we must share it as widely as possible.

It is important also to remember that we are called to the kingdom and the kingdom places some unique requirements upon the kingdom individual. No success criterion must ever be allowed to erase the demands of the kingdom. Citizenship is based upon some prior commitments to those demands. One can grow in citizenship after he or she has become a citizen, but one must not be invited to citizenship on false pretenses.

When all is said and done, we do have to remember that the church is not like any other institution. There are no "scientific techniques" that can guarantee its growth. There is a call of Christ and an inspiration of the Spirit that are beyond any technique, that shape themselves beyond any hard and fast forms, and that are impervious to human analysis. Hard-working and diligent and wise we must be, but ultimately we are not the key to God's success.

Notes

Introduction: A Setting and a Hope

[1] C. Peter Wagner, *Your Church Can Grow* (Glendale, Calif.: Regal Books, a div. of G/L Publications, 1976), p. 10. Used by permission.

[2] Donald A. McGavran, *Understanding Church Growth* (Grand Rapids, Mich.: Wm. B. Eerdmans Publishing Company, 1970).

[3] Robert Schuller, *Your Church Has Real Possibilities* (Glendale, Calif.: Regal Books, a div. of G/L Publications, 1975).

[4] Wagner, *op. cit.*, p. 18.

[5] I was dismissed from Midwestern Baptist Theological Seminary in Kansas City, Missouri, because of controversy centered in my book, *The Message of Genesis* (Nashville: Broadman Press, 1961).

[6] Donald A. McGavran, quoted by C. Peter Wagner, *Our Kind of People: The Ethical Dimension of Church Growth in America* (Atlanta: John Knox Press, 1979), p. 1. Copyright 1979 John Knox Press, Used by permission.

[7] Donald A. McGavran and Winfield C. Arn, *How to Grow a Church* (Glendale, Calif.: Regal Books, a div. of G/L Publications, 1973), p. 9.

[8] Robert K. Hudnut, *Church Growth Is Not the Point* (New York: Harper & Row, Publishers, Inc., 1975), p. ix.

Chapter 1: A Theology of Church and Mission

[1] George E. Mendenhall, *Law and Covenant in Israel and the Ancient Near East* (Pittsburgh: The Biblical Colloquium, 1955). I am essentially following his delineation.

[2] See Robert Schuller, *Your Church Has Real Possibilities* (Glendale, Calif.: Regal Books, a div. of G/L Publications, 1975).

[3] José de Broucker, *Dom Helder Camara: The Conversions of a Bishop*, trans. Hilary Davis (Glasgow: William Collins Sons and Co., Ltd., 1979), p. 173.

Chapter 2: An Analysis of Church Growth in Light of a Theological Understanding of the Church

[1]Charles L. Chaney and Ron S. Lewis, *Design for Church Growth* (Nashville: Broadman Press, 1978), p. 117. All rights reserved. Used by permission.

[2]Donald A. McGavran and Winfield C. Arn, *How to Grow a Church* (Glendale, Calif.: Regal Books, a div. of G/L Publications, 1973), p. 12. Copyright1973, Regal Books, Ventura CA 93066. Used by permission.

[3]As reported in Charles Mylander, *Secrets for Growing Churches* (San Francisco: Harper & Row, Publishers, Inc., 1979), p. 26.

[4]McGavran and Arn, *op. cit.*, pp. 2-3.

[5]Mylander, *op. cit.*, pp. 27-41.

[6]Chaney and Lewis, *op. cit.*, p. 30.

[7]*Ibid.*, p. 31.

[8]*Ibid.*

[9]*Ibid.*

[10]Richard Sprague, *McCall's*, March, 1977, p. 158, as quoted by Chaney and Lewis, *op. cit.*, p. 34.

[11]Donald A. McGavran and Winfield C. Arn, *Ten Steps for Church Growth* (San Francisco: Harper & Row, Publishers, Inc., 1977), p. 22.

[12]Mylander, *op. cit.*, p. viii.

[13]Chaney and Lewis, *op. cit.*, p. 16.

[14]*Ibid.*, p. 18.

[15]*Ibid.*

[16]*Ibid.*

[17]Mylander, *op. cit.*, p. 41.

[18]McGavran and Arn, *Ten Steps for Church Growth*, p. 69.

[19]C. Peter Wagner, *Your Spiritual Gifts Can Help Your Church Grow* (Glendale, Calif.: Regal Books, a div. of G/L Publications, 1979), p. 196.

[20]Mylander, *op. cit.*, p. 43.

[21]*Ibid.*, p. 44.

[22]Chaney and Lewis, *op. cit.*, p. 144.

[23]Wagner, *Your Spiritual Gifts Can Help Your Church Grow*, p. 196.

[24]Mylander, *op. cit.*, p. 45.

[25]McGavran and Arn, *Ten Steps for Church Growth*, p. 21.

[26]*Ibid.*, p. 20.

[27]*Ibid.*, p. 26.

[28]*Ibid.*, pp. 26-30.

[29]Alan R. Tippitt, *Church Growth and the Word of God* (Grand Rapids, Mich.: Wm. B. Eerdmans Publishing Company, 1970), pp. 48-50.

[30]McGavran and Arn, *How to Grow a Church*, p. 42.

[31]McGavran and Arn, *Ten Steps for Church Growth*, p. 20.

[32]Chaney and Lewis, *op. cit.*, p. 29.

[33]*Ibid.*, p. 26.

[34]*Ibid.*, p. 76.

[35]Tippitt, *op. cit.*, p. 39.

[36]Wagner, *Your Church Can Grow*, p..51.

[37]McGavran and Arn, *Ten Steps for Church Growth*, p. 9.

[38]George G. Hunter III, *The Contagious Congregation* (Nashville: Abingdon Press, 1979), p. 19.

[39] Herodotus, as quoted by McGavran and Arn in *Ten Steps for Church Growth*, p. 123.

[40] Tippitt, *op. cit.*, p. 18, using material from a Doctor of Ministry thesis at Fuller Theological Seminary, "Church Growth and Church Health: Diagnosis and Prescription," by David W. Bennett and James E. Murphy.

[41] Chaney and Lewis, *op. cit.*, p. 56.

[42] *Ibid.*

[43] McGavran and Arn, *Ten Steps for Church Growth*, p. 104.

[44] Mylander, *op. cit.*, p. 62.

[45] Wagner, *Your Spiritual Gifts Can Help Your Church Grow*, p. 177. Used by permission.

[46] *Ibid.*, p. 252.

[47] Orlando E. Costas, *The Integrity of Mission: The Inner Life and Outreach of the Church* (San Francisco: Harper & Row, Publishers, Inc., 1979), p. 26.

[48] *Ibid.*, p. 27.

[49] *Ibid.*, p. 32.

[50] Mylander, *op. cit.*, pp. 58-60.

[51] Hunter, *op. cit.*, p. 26.

[52] *Ibid.*, p. 28.

[53] *Ibid.*, pp. 30-31.

[54] *Ibid.*, p. 30.

[55] McGavran and Arn, *Ten Steps for Church Growth*, pp. 55-56.

[56] McGavran and Arn, *How to Grow a Church*, pp. 82-88.

[57] McGavran and Arn, *Ten Steps for Church Growth*, p. 50.

[58] *Ibid.*

[59] Donald A. McGavran, *Understanding Church Growth* (Grand Rapids, Mich.: Wm. B. Eerdmans Publishing Company, 1970), p. 198.

[60] C. Peter Wagner, *Our Kind of People: The Ethical Dimensions of Church Growth in America* (Atlanta: John Knox Press, 1979), pp. 104ff.

[61] *Ibid.*, p. 21. Copyright 1979 John Knox Press. Used by permission.

[62] *Ibid.*, pp. 23-26.

[63] McGavran, *op. cit.*, p. 44.

[64] *Ibid.*, p. 56.

[65] McGavran and Arn, *Ten Steps for Church Growth*, p. 11.

[66] Costas, *op. cit.*, p. 16.

[67] Chaney and Lewis, *op. cit.*, p. 57.

[68] Wagner, *Your Spiritual Gifts Can Help Your Church Grow*, p. 108.

[69] *Ibid.*, p. 32.

[70] *Ibid.*, p. 41.

[71] McGavran and Arn, *How to Grow a Church*, p. 33.

[72] Dietrich Bonhoeffer, *Life Together*, trans. John W. Doberstein (New York: Harper & Row, Publishers, Inc., 1954), p. 77.

[73] *Ibid.*

[74] *Ibid.*

[75] McGavran and Arn, *Ten Steps for Church Growth*, p. 30.

Chapter 3: An Evaluation of the Church Growth Movement

[1] Orlando E. Costas, *The Integrity of Mission: The Inner Life and Outreach*

of the Church (San Francisco: Harper & Row, Publishers, Inc., 1979), pp. 37-60.

[2] Donald A. McGavran and Win C. Arn, *How to Grow a Church* (Glendale, Calif.: Regal Books, a div. of G/L Publications, 1973), pp. 34-35.

[3] See McGavran's quote in C. Peter Wagner, *Our Kind of People: The Ethical Dimensions of Church Growth in America* (Atlanta: John Knox Press, 1979), p. 21.

[4] J. Robertson McQuilkin, *How Biblical Is the Church Growth Movement?* now retitled *Measuring the Church Growth Movement* (Chicago: Moody Press, 1973, 1974), p. 9.

[5] Cf. discussion in *ibid.*, pp. 19-20, where McQuilkin treats very unfavorably the material of C. René Padilla, "A Steep Climb Ahead for Theology in Latin America," from *Evangelical Missions Quarterly*, vol. 7, no. 2 (Winter, 1971), pp. 102, 104-105.

[6] Wagner, *Our Kind of People*, p. 112. Copyright 1979 John Knox Press. Used by permission.

[7] *Ibid.*, p. 118.

[8] *Ibid.*

[9] Harold E. Bauman, "Goals of Church Growth," in *Missions, Evangelism, and Church Growth*, ed. C. Norman Kraus (Scottsdale, Pa.: Herald Press, 1980), p. 152.

[10] Wagner, *Our Kind of People*, p. 104.

[11] Carl S. Dudley, *Where Have All Our People Gone? New Choices for Old Churches* (New York: The Pilgrim Press, 1979), p. 57.

[12] McGavran and Arn, *How to Grow a Church*, p. 31.

[13] Donald A. McGavran and Winfield C. Arn, *Ten Steps for Church Growth* (San Francisco: Harper & Row, Publishers, Inc., 1977), p. 40.

[14] Charles Mylander, *Secrets for Growing Churches* (San Francisco: Harper & Row, Publishers, Inc., 1979), p. 129.

[15] *Ibid.*, p. 136.

[16] *Ibid.*, p. 82.

[17] C. Peter Wagner, *Your Church Can Grow* (Glendale, Calif.: Regal Books, a div. of G/L Publications, 1976), p. 158. Used by permission.

[18] *Ibid.*, p. 159.

[19] Alan R. Tippitt, *Church Growth and the Word of God* (Grand Rapids, Mich.: Wm. B. Eerdmans Publishing Company, 1970), pp. 54-57.

[20] Wagner, *Your Church Can Grow*, p. 148.

[21] Cf. the permeating philosophy and counsel to pastors in the book used in connection with the pastors' institutes at Garden Grove: Robert Schuller, *Your Church Has Real Possibilities* (Glendale, Calif.: Regal Books, a div. of G/L Publications, 1975).

[22] José de Broucker, *Dom Helder Camara: The Conversions of a Bishop*, trans. Hilary Davis (Glasgow: William Collins Sons and Co., Ltd., 1979).

[23] Much of this discussion was germinated by James Limburg in *The Prophets and the Powerless* (Atlanta: John Knox Press, 1976).

[24] John Killinger, *A Devotional Guide to Luke: The Gospel of Contagious Joy* (Waco, Tex.: Word, Inc., 1980), p. 12.

[25] Alvin C. Porteous, *Preaching to Suburban Captives* (Valley Forge: Judson Press, 1979), p. 119.

[26] Walter Rauschenbusch, *A Theology for the Social Gospel* (New York: Macmillan, Inc., 1917), pp. 98-101.

[27] Costas, *op. cit.,* p. 75.

[28] Bauman, "Goals of Church Growth," in Kraus, *op. cit.,* p. 157.

[29] Ralph H. Elliott, *Reconciliation and the New Age* (Valley Forge: Judson Press, 1973).

[30] John H. Yoder, "Church Growth Issues in Theological Perspective," in *The Challenge of Church Growth,* ed. Wilbert R. Shenk (Scottsdale, Pa.: Herald Press, 1973), pp. 31-35.

[31] *Ibid.,* p. 29.

[32] C. Peter Wagner, *Your Spiritual Gifts Can Help Your Church Grow* (Glendale, Calif.: Regal Books, a div. of G/L Publications, 1979), pp. 246-247.

[33] Mylander, *op. cit.,* p. viii.

[34] Charles L. Chaney and Ron S. Lewis, *Design for Church Growth* (Nashville: Broadman Press, 1978), p. 29.

[35] Donald A. McGavran, *Understanding Church Growth* (Grand Rapids, Mich.: Wm. B. Eerdmans Publishing Company, 1970), pp. 45, 44.

[36] *Ibid.,* pp. 216-232.

[37] Tippitt, *op. cit.,* p. 52.

[38] Robert L. Ramseyer, "Anthropological Perspectives on Church Growth," in Shenk, *op. cit.,* p. 67.

[39] *Ibid.,* p. 45.

[40] McGavran and Arn, *How to Grow a Church,* p. 27.

[41] Gibson Winter, *The Suburban Captivity of the Churches* (New York: Macmillan, Inc., 1962), p. 68.

[42] Donald W. Shriver, Jr., and Karl A. Ostrom, *Is There Hope for the City?* (Philadelphia: The Westminster Press, 1977), p. 10.

[43] Vern L. Miller, "Evangelizing the Central City: Problems and Possibilities," in Kraus, *op. cit.,* p. 129.

[44] See James D. Smart, *The Cultural Subversion of the Biblical Faith* (Philadelphia: The Westminster Press, 1977).

[45] See Jacques Ellul, *The Meaning of the City,* trans. Dennis Pardee (Grand Rapids, Mich.: Wm. B. Eerdmans Publishing Company, 1970).

[46] McGavran and Arn, *Ten Steps for Church Growth,* p. 6.

[47] Cf. especially the correspondence between Donald McGavran and Victor E. W. Hayward as summarized and reported under the title "Without Crossing Barriers? One in Christ vs. Discipling Diverse Cultures," found in *Missiology: An International Review,* vol. II, April, 1974, pp. 203-224.

[48] Yoder in Shenk, *op. cit.,* p. 28.

[49] Allen H. Howe, "The Church: Its Growth and Mission" in Shenk, *op. cit.,* p. 62.

[50] Mylander, *op. cit.,* p. 136.

[51] These quoted terms, exclusive of each other, are used in McGavran and Arn, *Ten Steps for Church Growth,* p. 5.

[52] Wagner, *Your Church Can Grow,* p. 57.

[53] *Ibid.,* p. 67.

[54] *Ibid.*

[55] Wagner, *Your Spiritual Gifts Can Help Your Church Grow,* pp. 249-250.

[56] *Ibid.,* p. 140.

[57] *Ibid.,* p. 143.

[58] *Ibid.*, p. 144.

[59] *Ibid.*, p. 152.

[60] *Ibid.*, p. 38.

[61] *Ibid.*, p. 249.

[62] McGavran and Arn, *How to Grow a Church,* p. 95.

[63] Wagner, *Your Spiritual Gifts Can Help Your Church Grow,* p. 176.

[64] Ralph H. Elliott, ''The Minister as Professional,'' *Foundations,* vol. 22, no. 2 (April–June, 1979), p. 118.

[65] Reuel Howe, *Partners in Preaching: Clergy and Laity in Dialogue* (New York: The Seabury Press, Inc., 1967), p. 42.

[66] Raymond Abba, *Principles of Christian Worship* (New York: Oxford University Press, 1957), p. 65.

[67] John Knox, *The Integrity of Preaching* (Nashville: Abingdon Press, 1957), pp. 94-95.

Chapter 4: A Positive Ministry for Growth

[1] Robert K. Hudnut, *Church Growth Is Not the Point* (New York: Harper & Row, Publishers, Inc., 1975), p. ix.

[2] Browne Barr, *Parish Backtalk* (New York: Abingdon Press, 1964), p. 66.

[3] Cf. Jitsuo Morikawa, *Biblical Dimensions of Church Growth* (Valley Forge: Judson Press, 1979).

[4] Carnegie Samuel Calian, *Today's Pastor in Tomorrow's World* (New York: E. P. Dutton and Elsevier Book Operations, 1977), pp. 8-22.

[5] Cf. *Ibid.*, in his reference to the work of management consultant Peter Drucker.

[6] *Ibid.*, p. 23.

[7] William J. Bouwsma; ''Christian Adulthood,'' *Daedelus,* Spring, 1976, p. 83, quoted by Calian, *op. cit.*, p. 73.

Chapter 5: The Shape of the Local Parish

[1] Gleanings from a presentation to the Official Board of North Shore Baptist Church by Dr. John Boyle, Director of the Lorene Replogle Counseling Center, June 10, 1980.

[2] Armand M. Nicholi, Jr., ed., *The Harvard Guide to Modern Psychiatry* (Cambridge, Mass.: Belknap Press of Harvard University Press, 1978).